Save the Kid!

How the Arrest of a January 6th Protester

Revealed a

Moral Compass That Can Save America.

By Reed K. Christensen

Copyright © 2021 by Reed Christensen

Save the Kid!

All rights reserved. No part of this publication may be reproduced, distributed, or transmitted in any form or by any means, including photocopying, recording, or other electronic or mechanical methods, without the prior written permission of the publisher, except in the case of brief quotations embodied in critical reviews and certain other noncommercial uses permitted by copyright law.

Although the author and publisher have made every effort to ensure the information in this book was correct at press time, the author and publisher do not assume and hereby disclaim any liability to any party for any loss, damage, or disruption caused by errors or omissions, whether such errors or omissions result from negligence, accident, or any other cause.

Neither the author nor the publisher assumes any responsibility or liability whatsoever on behalf of the consumer or reader of this material. The experiences and opinions in this book are given to provide the personal beliefs of the author and to reveal the origin and workings of a moral compass. Neither the author nor the publisher can be held responsible for the use of the information provided within this book as individuals shape their own moral beliefs and actions.

All copyrighted or trademarked company names referenced in the text are the property of their respective owners.

ISBN: 979-8-9854755-0-0 (paperback)
ISBN: 979-8-9854755-1-7 (hardback)
ISBN: 979-8-9854755-2-4 (E-book)
ISBN: 979-8-9854755-3-1 (Audiobook)

Dedication

To my parents, Gary and Lorene Christensen, who through word and deed taught me about love of God, Country, and Family.

To my wife, Myra, whom I loved from the first moment I saw her, as I stood by the dessert table at a church dance, at the age of seventeen.

Contents

Foreword..9
Introduction..11

I. People on the Sidewalk

Chapter 1 – The Arrest..15
Chapter 2 – The Hearing...31
Chapter 3 – The Greenhorn Protesters.................................39
Chapter 4 – What does it Mean?...43
Chapter 5 – America in the Street...47

II. Outcomes of Obedience

Chapter 6 – The Good...53
Chapter 7 – The Bad...57
Chapter 8 – The Ugly..61
Chapter 9 – The Ugly Comes Home.....................................67

III. Using an Inner Moral Compass

Chapter 10 – Be Law Abiding, Right?..................................75
Chapter 11 – The Need for a Compass.................................77
Chapter 12 – Finding the Right Compass.............................79

IV. The Constitution as Compass

Chapter 13 – Principles of Freedom.....................................87
Chapter 14 – Reading the Compass......................................95

V. Being a Moral Actor

Chapter 15 – I Don't do That...111
Chapter 16 – I Should do That...119
Chapter 17 – Finding the Courage.......................................125

Endnotes...137

Foreword

This book is addressed to those Americans who believe in the beauty and wonder of the Constitution. The hope is it will inspire them to find a path through the chaos of our current political landscape so America can be preserved in full measure for future generations.

The references in this book are intended to be sufficient for such a reader as described above. Comments on the current political situations in America or historical events that are well-known and accepted by the Right are not heavily referenced.

The reason for this one-sided nature of the book is I am quite sure it is beyond my ability to list references to convince fellow citizens who hate America that its founding was a miracle of the ages. This inability was made clear when I first started out and was attempting to reference current events and found that all news articles fell into distinct "us" or "them" outlets.

This resignation was recently further reinforced while reading a news report about people who call themselves "Antifa" (anti-fascists) dressing in black, showing their support for the power of the state to make sweeping medical mandates by beating medical-freedom protesters whose beliefs were deemed to be politically unacceptable. What I took from this report is, today in America, we cannot agree on even the definition of words. A very serious split has occurred—indeed our society is divided by a frightening chasm—when one side's values cause it to choose the prefix *anti* where I would choose the prefix *hyper*.

Introduction

As officers approached the car on both sides, I lowered my window on the passenger side. A male deputy on the passenger side announced, "I have a warrant for the arrest of Reed Christensen."

I turned to my wife and said, "It's because I'm a Trump supporter."

Thus began my arrest by the FBI and my entanglement in the Federal legal system with hearings held in the Courts of the District of Oregon and the District of Columbia for my actions at the Stop the Steal rally on January 6, 2021 in Washington DC.

This book tells my story of the Rally, my arrest and imprisonment, my initial hearing, and the story of how a rally many years ago here in the Portland area prompted the realization of a moral truth.

It is my hope and prayer that good people will use this truth as a moral compass, a guide in contentious times, to save the miraculous promise that is America.

I. People on the Sidewalk

Chapter 1 – The Arrest

The last week of April 2021 was a week that changed everything in my life.

On Sunday April 25th, my wife and I were following our normal routine—we had dressed in our good clothes and settled in the car at about 1:30pm to head to church. My wife was in the driver's seat; she had been doing all the driving since my stroke at the end of January. The stroke had happened just a few months before my 63rd birthday. I had spent three weeks in the hospital and ten days in rehab learning how to walk again—and although by then I was walking without a walker or cane, she was leery my driving would be as wobbly as my walking.

As we drove through our rural neighborhood, located amid active farmland in the Willamette Valley of Oregon, we noticed a couple of sheriff cars and other vehicles clustered on a side street we passed. We both wondered aloud about what could be going on at the neighbors' for multiple sheriff cars to be involved.

As we proceeded up the road, a sheriff car pulled behind us and then, shortly after, flipped on its lights. I commented to my wife that she must have been driving too fast!

She pulled over. As officers approached the car on both sides, I lowered my window on the passenger side. A male deputy on the passenger side announced, "I have a warrant for the arrest of Reed Christensen."[i]

I turned to my wife and said, "It's because I'm a Trump supporter."

We were both calm, with a feeling of resignation, like we had just experienced the arrival of a brutal storm that we had been tracking that had been stuck on the horizon. A friend had told us weeks before that a picture of me at the January 6th Washington DC rally was on the FBI website asking the public for help in identification. It was back at that point Myra had cried, had panic attacks where she could hardly breathe, and had spent sleepless nights even after using sleep aid medication. I hadn't been too excited at the news. After college I spent four years active duty in the Army, and had some experience with the Federal government. I had a lot of faith in the government's ability to mess up, be inefficient, and take forever to do anything. Also, being a somewhat introverted engineer, I had no social media presence—and, as far as I knew, there was just one picture of me on the web at the Washington County Republican website.

The deputy walked me to the back of our car.

"Can I go home and get my MAGA hat before you throw me to the ground?" I asked.

Not responding to that, he asked me to confirm my name, date of birth, and the last four digits of my Social Security number, which I did.

"Do you have anything in your pockets?" he continued.

"Just this stuff," I replied as I handed over a chapstick, fingernail clippers, and a handkerchief. I was not carrying my

THE ARREST

wallet or keys as I was not driving. As we stood and he cuffed my hands behind my back, I told him, "I know I am a political prisoner for being a Trump supporter who went to the January 6th Rally, and I will not talk to anyone other than my lawyer."

I don't remember hearing any response to that either.

While I was being processed and cuffed, I looked over and saw Myra standing outside the driver's door surrounded by a uniformed deputy and two or three plainclothes officers with "FBI" on their jackets. She told me later that after demanding to see an arrest warrant, she was shown a stack of documents with the warrant, the charges against me, and an incredibly high-resolution aerial image of the farm, way better than the view from zooming in on Google maps. She also saw annotations on the image, adding details that could only be known from someone who had been at the site on the ground. She was also quite emphatic in emphasizing that my health was of great concern and I was on four medications while coping with the aftermath of a major stroke.

The whole experience was not like the dramatic arrests you see in videos. No throwing to the ground or to the car hood, or even any harshness or rancor. As I thought about it later, you could say the arrest was exactly like one would expect from officers trying to be "Oregon decent," picking up a guy who they knew was not dangerous, who laid in wait to pick him up knowing every week at this time he dressed in a suit on his way to church with his wife.

As I was hauled away to a jail cell, my wife was taken back to our home to watch fifteen FBI agents trample through our property at the end of a quiet road, which had been our peaceful sanctuary in the country for over twenty years. They confiscated my stroke medication, my cell phone and work laptop, and some of my clothes. Myra assisted with the search for specific clothing items that I had worn at the January 6th Rally, like the Marmot brand gray rain coat, hiking boots, and yellow leather work gloves (they took a new package with four sets of gloves). They didn't take my red MAGA hat, which I had worn at the Rally that day. It was in my office in a plastic tub of political items where I kept material for my work as Secretary of the Washington County GOP. My wife did see them sorting through paperwork in my office. A later review of security camera footage showed agents with M4 rifles were out in the barnyard checking the out buildings, while Myra was repeatedly asked, "where are all the guns?" Her requests to see a search warrant were denied until, after persisting for over an hour, she was finally shown the warrant.

And yet the Federal government's incarceration plan for me, the guy whose arresting charges my wife saw included two counts of "walking on the grass," went awry from the very beginning. It started when the arresting deputy did not think it was important to tell anyone at the county jail that I thought I was a political prisoner and would not talk to anyone, for the jail staff all proceeded to question me and expect answers.

Entering the jail, I was sat on a steel bench with my hands still cuffed behind my back at the jail in-processing desk.

"What is your name?" a female deputy asked.

I did not respond, although, I did think, *Why did you arrest me if you weren't sure who I am?* As several other administrative questions were asked, I looked blankly at her, not even moving my head to answer yes/no type questions. She called for help and a group of male deputies came over, stood me up and faced me to the wall. They patted down my suit, and then turned me around. Several questions were tossed out, none of which I answered.

Finally, the deputy taking the lead said, "If you do not answer my question about feeling suicidal, we will assume you are and will strip you down and put you into a holding cell. Do you want that to happen?"

I spoke no answer and gave no physical response.

I was taken across the hallway to a small cinder block cell just barely wider than the door, with a concrete bench off to the side of the door, and a waist-high cinder block wall toward the back that offered minimal privacy for a stainless steel toilet with a drinking faucet on the back tank. At least three deputies were present standing in the open doorway.

My handcuffs were removed, and a deputy ordered, "Take off all your clothes."

I unclothed silently, handing each clothing item over to be placed into a plastic bag. I then stood naked facing the doorway.

"Raise your arms. Show either side of your scrotum. Turn around. Bend over and use your hands to pull your cheeks apart." After complying with the verbal cavity search, the deputy said, "Here, put on this smock."

I was handed an unfamiliar article made of padded material. I turned it over and over, trying to figure out what it was and how it should be worn. A deputy reached out for the smock and placed it over my head, fastening the shoulder tabs that were fixed with velcro. Immediately the velcro fasteners gave way and the garment fell down around my ankles. At that, the deputies left the doorway and closed the door. I picked up the garment and wrapped it around my waist in the form of a lava-lava, grasping it with one hand and sat down on the concrete bench. My prison "skirt" insulated me from the cold, bare concrete bench, and even though I was bare chested and bare legged with no socks, the temperature was bearable.

I had no sight of a clock, but two times I saw a deputy come, peer through the door window, and then write on a pad attached to the wall next to the door, at an interval I judged to be thirty minutes. After this a deputy came with a clipboard, propped the door open with his foot, and said that I needed to fill out a form. I did not respond, verbally or physically. He then began a stream of questions.

"Mr. Reed, what is your middle initial?" "Mr. Reed, what is your address?" "Don't you want to talk to me?"

The tone of the questioning was low key and calm—but it was incessant. It droned on and on, repeating the questions over and over without stopping, for what I judged to be an hour. I sat non-responsive and looked ahead.

THE ARREST

While the door was open, a woman dressed in hospital scrubs came over and poked her head between the open door and the questioning deputy. She was holding pill bottles in her hand.

"We just received these medications for you, what are they for?"

I replied, "They are my stroke medications. I am recovering from having a major stroke, which I had at the end of January."

She seemed content at that, nodded, and left. I had no reluctance in talking to a nurse—it was the officers processing a political prisoner that I had a problem with, and it didn't help my attitude toward them that they were all dressed in black uniforms.

I had a brief thought that the stroke revelation I spoke to the nurse might cause my interrogating jailer to reconsider the wisdom of putting a gray-haired guy naked in a holding cell. I was beginning to shiver as it was chilly with the door open and colder air from the main jail hallway was coming in. But the deputy started up his questions, in the same manner as before.

"Do you still live at 1234?" "What does the K stand for in your middle name?"

So that was the game! I realized there was no urgent form that required filling out to gather important unknown information. They knew every bit of information that I had been asked for two hours. It was an obedience ploy. Start with something small and innocuous for the recalcitrant prisoner to obey—"fill out this form." It was to be the beginning of my obedience training. This realization put me on the alert for other prisoner-control methods. I immediately determined to never ask for anything from a jailer. I knew from my reading of histories that asking for something could be used as leverage against me—if you want that, you have to do this. This was the reason I never made a phone call from the jail. I had decided against it, because a female deputy had placed a phone card on the bench, saying that I could make a call—if I asked.

It felt weird to be recognizing and worrying about prison procedures, this from a a guy who only ever had a couple of driving tickets. But I was an avid history reader and had read a lot about the camps and gulags of the German and Soviet Socialists—and now I was a political prisoner! I suspected the deputies in this county jail were just mechanically following local checklists and procedures, but I decided I needed to use what I knew of political prisons to get mentally ready for when I was transferred over to the police state big leagues – the FBI and the Federal legal system.

At the end of two hours of interrogation, a deputy came by the holding cell with a jug and paper cups and asked if I would like something to drink. It was near 5pm, and I had not had a drink all afternoon, so I took a chance and said yes. I was relieved when without comment he promptly filled up the cup twice for me.

"Can I keep the cup?" I asked.

"Yes," he said.

I had found it was impossible to drink enough water from the dribble coming from the drinking faucet on the back of the toilet. Using the paper cup helped me down some significant water. Soon after this a deputy came to escort me back out to the in-processing area of the jail. I was not chained as I held the smock with one hand and walked barefoot and bare chested to the mug shot stand. The processing deputy thought it would not be good to have me bare chested in the photo, so he found a shirt and threw it over my front and it covered my neck and shoulders.

"You are going to be put into a suicide observation cell. You need medical in-processing and a psychiatric evaluation," a deputy said.

He led me barefoot and bare chested holding my lava-lava to the nurses' station. The escorting deputy stood in the doorway while I sat in a chair right inside the room. The nurse there asked me to fill out a medical release form by using my fingernail to sign on a wired pad.

I replied, "I am a political prisoner. And I will not sign anything when you have not shown me a document, and I do not know where my signature is going."

She searched around her desk and came up with a paper copy of the medical release. I read the form, asked for a pen, and signed it. We had a discussion about my four stroke medications, which she typed into the computer.

"The doctor is trying to keep my blood pressure under 130 / 80," I said. She put a cuff on my left arm, and pressed the button on the machine. I watched the machine readout; when it stopped it said 210 / 101.

"Whoa! That can't be right!", the nurse exclaimed as she leaped out of her chair and faced the machine. "We'll try it again." She got a bigger sized cuff and put it on my right arm. This time the reading was 183 / 90. She seemed satisfied with that and recorded it.

I knew those readings were bad. When I was hospitalized with my stroke, a roommate had a blood-pressure reading that came in as 190 over something. Immediately, a couple of doctors and two or three nurses swarmed into the room and began to do mitigation activities.

"Will you please help me?" I asked the nurse. "I have just had a stroke and I know those readings are bad." "They are planning to take me and put me naked into an observation cell for the night." "They say they are doing this because I was unresponsive about a question about suicide, but I am most emphatically *not* suicidal." "I also will not answer any other psychiatric evaluation questions because I am a political prisoner."

"The deputies know what they are doing," she said with an expression that conveyed to me that she knew she was a small cog in a big machine.

I tried to reply, but it was evident that she had turned off, so I just said, "Never mind."

I was given a pair of slip-on canvas shoes and led to the observation block, and the shoes were taken back when we arrived. I was assigned to cell #21, and as I approached the door, a deputy motioned at a smock thrown over a rack and said I might try that one to see if it stayed fastened. I grabbed at the smock, taking it with me while keeping my fist on the lava-lava. I was having difficulty keeping warm with just one smock to cover me, so I was pleased at the thought of having two for the night.

The cell was quite large, with a prison toilet behind a waist high cinder block wall in the middle and rooms that looked to be 10' by 10' on each side. A small metal sink with a drinking faucet was on the wall in the left room, with nothing else in the room. The sink had bits of debris around the sink handles and in the sink bowl. I couldn't tell if the debris was food or vomit residue. A drinking faucet was on the right side of the sink bowl. The room with the sink was littered with small debris that appeared to be orange cracker crumbs. The right side of the room had no furniture, bed, blanket, or pillow. The only furnishing is what looked like a six-foot-long blue plastic doggie bed on the floor. It had foam edging covered with plastic around the sides, except for a gap at the near side. The foam sleeping mat in the middle was still thickened on the ends but crushed flat in the center. The doggie bed too was covered with orange crumbs. I brushed it off the best I could and plopped down naked on it. I opened the torso velcro fastener that ran the front length on the smocks and used them as blankets—one to cover my legs and the other to cover my shoulders.

Strangely enough, I was glad to be there. When I was at home, I would still get tired while recovering from the stroke and would take an afternoon nap, so it had been a long afternoon for me. I was tired, my head was hurting, and it felt good to lie down in my own space with no one around.

The first visitors I heard were two people in medical scrubs who knocked and said, "We are here with your meds." They handed me a dixie cup through the door slit that contained my blood thinner and blood-pressure pills.

"What time is it?" I asked.

"It is 8pm."

"My regular nightly routine is to take two tablets or 10mg of Baclofen at night to control diaphragm spasms," I informed them. "It was among my stroke medication. Can you get me some?"

"We will have to check with the provider," came the reply.

"Can I keep the cup for water?" I asked.

"No, that is against the rules."

I handed the cup back through the door slit. The medication people never came back. I was dreading the return of the intense spasms in my diaphragm that had occurred after my stroke while I was in the hospital. They had come every seven seconds without stopping for three days until the doctors figured out the right medicine and dosage to calm down my breathing.

The remainder of the night passed without outside interruption. I had to get up frequently to urinate—it seemed like every hour. I figured my body was running faster to generate heat, as I could barely keep covered, and that was only when in a fetal position. I didn't care too much about the frequent toilet trips because I was unable to sleep the entire night. A fluorescent light glared in the cell until it dimmed a bit at what I assumed was 10pm. It was definitely not the absolute quiet and darkness I was used to in my bedroom at home in the country. I constantly shifted position from left side to right side to back to relieve pressure. I had a headache, and my right arm, which had been "asleep" for three months since the stroke, throbbed painfully. Every time I got up to urinate with nothing on but a smock over my shoulders, I would sip water from the faucet. But I could tell I was not replacing enough water from sipping at the dribbling from the faucet. The one bright spot in the night was I only had a few occasional hiccups, nothing like my original diaphragm spasms.

To bolster my morale, I mouthed some memorized hymns from church—after all it was Sunday evening. My throat was too dry to actually sing. I did a lot of praying—being especially worried due to my high blood pressure and my recent stroke. Myra had taken my stroke really hard. My body type and build takes after my Mom's side of the family, and my Mom's downward spiral and eventual death had started with a massive stroke less than two years before. Her dad had died of a stroke, and his dad had also. Myra told me that she had been resigned to the fact she would be left alone, telling me that one of the things she had worried about was she couldn't stay on our 16-acre property without me. I had been bouncing back pretty well, but now I was sick at the thought of her having to deal with me having another stroke, or me dying from one.

Toward morning I heard a loud voice bark a question outside my cell. The words of the question did not register and I wasn't sure it was directed at me. The question came loudly again; this time I understood.

"Do you want breakfast; yes or no?"

I was lying with my face away from the door, so I twisted around to see who was asking. I could see the black uniform of a deputy through the door window with the door slit open. Given that I was determined not to express any needs to a jailer, I silently turned away and laid back down. The metal slot in the door loudly slammed shut.

Around 8am, a two-person nurse team came around with my medications. Again the medications were incomplete with no dosage of Baclofen for spasms. I explained that my evening medications were wrong too and asked if I could get my usual pills.

Again the response came, "It is up to the provider."

At this point I was totally exasperated and caustically replied, "If you were real nurses, you would call someone and report elder abuse."

Around 9am a deputy opened the door to my cell and threw in a bright yellow prison jumpsuit.

"Put it on," he ordered.

Just minutes later, I was taken to the main desk area at the jail entrance. I was put in an ankle chain and a torso chain which the deputy cinched tightly up against my diaphragm. I was then turned over to the custody of a man and a woman dressed in plain clothes; I presumed they were marshals. They led me outside, and as I climbed into the passenger-side back seat of a black SUV, a sudden searing pain shot up my right side. I grimaced and gasped for air but could not get anything into my lungs.

"Are you okay?" "Can you breathe?" the marshals asked.

I shook my head, not saying anything as they grabbed me and yanked me back out of the car. They loosened the torso chain, and we all got in and drove in silence to downtown Portland. The car turned into an underground parking garage where I was turned over to a couple of jailers in green khaki pants and light green t-shirts. These men removed the torso chain and replaced my leg chain with ankle cuffs tethered with a short chain. They escorted me to a large holding cell with white painted benches on each side of the wall, which had been heavily scratched up with graffiti, and a prison toilet behind a low cinder block wall at the back.

I had arrived at the Portland Federal Building, home of the FBI and Federal court system in Oregon.

SAVE THE KID!

Chapter 2 – The Hearing

The great thing about being a recovering stroke patient and spending the night naked in a Washington County observation cell for being silent, is at my hearing the following day, the Oregon based Federal judge was not very happy about how I was treated.

After a short time a jailer arrived and escorted me to an in-processing room. I had a picture taken and started the process of taking electronic scans of each of my fingertips.

The jailer taking my prints noticed my silence and commented, "You know, we are not FBI agents."

At that I decided to talk, and we had a back-and-forth discussion about the fingerprinting process, as it kept failing and had to be retried.

"This is typical lowest-bidder government software," the jailer complained.

Finally after completing the scans, I was taken back to a holding cell.

I sat in the holding cell until a jailer came to escort me to a small room with a counter and a glass pane that divided the room in half. There was a stool on my side of the counter, and the glass pane had a small slot at the bottom. On the other side of the glass was a small notebook computer, the screen of which had a Zoom call that showed the face of a woman. She informed me she was a court-appointed attorney.

She started rattling off a laundry list of legal decisions I needed to consider and to which I needed to reply. The list was rattled off pretty quickly and perfunctorily, so I didn't really grasp anything.

"I didn't understand any of that," I rasped. I had trouble speaking because I was dehydrated. "I have not eaten or slept in 24 hours, and I am not feeling or thinking well."

That caused her to once more start mechanically rattling off the legal decisions I was required to make.

"Look, I have not yet even spoken to my wife." "I am not going to make any legal decisions when I can barely think," I said in exasperation.

"I can give her a call." "What is her number?" she asked as she pulled out a cell phone on the screen.

My wife answered her phone, and the woman introduced herself as my lawyer.

"Who did you vote for?" Myra asked forcefully.

"I'm not going to tell you that!" the woman replied. "But I assure you I can do my job impartially as a defender."

"Your answer tells me everything I need to know," Myra said. "We have retained our own lawyer, and he is on his way to the Federal Building right now."

THE HEARING

Myra and I exchanged a few words through the Zoom link, and the lady lawyer closed the Zoom connection. Almost immediately, the lawyer Myra had arranged entered through the door on the other side of the glass.

I was surprised at how much of a relief it was to see and talk to a sympathetic person. In the past, after we had heard of the FBI Wanted notice, and I had thought about the possibility of being caught up in the Federal legal system, I had figured I would not hire a lawyer. I had read of many cases where Federal court actions had dragged on for years—with no attempt at justice, just the obvious goal of the government to drain the financial life out of the defendant. I had a good job as an engineer doing processor development for Intel, but I could see that same thing easily happening to us. But it was definitely comforting to talk to someone who was there to help. I told him who I was, what I had done, and what I had just been through.

My detention hearing was a virtual Zoom meeting, held in the afternoon at 1:45pm, with Judge Youlee Yim You presiding.[ii] I sat on a metal stool, with my ankle cuffs and bright yellow jumpsuit looking into a laptop computer on a table in a narrow cement block hallway of the jail.

On the Zoom screen was the face of a female judge in a black robe. There were several other panes in the meeting, some had faces, but others were blank. The panes had labels under them like: "court clerk," "federal prosecutor," "pretrial release," etc. The hearing was delayed a bit until my lawyer was able to call in on the meeting with his phone.

At this point, it had been over 24 hours since I had slept, eaten, or had sufficient water to drink, so the legal discussions about a future identification hearing and court venues were confusing for me.

But I caught the exchange right at the beginning when the judge asked, "Do we also have a representative from Pretrial Services by telephone?"

The Pretrial lady responded, "Yes, your Honor. I was able to speak with the defendant's wife after providing the courts with the Pretrial Services report, and while I wasn't able to obtain as much information as we typically would verify, I do have enough information that we—Pretrial—does recommend release."

I wasn't sure the judge was too impressed by that recommendation, as she immediately moved on to other legal issues.

After a while she began to give a speech, "Mr. Christensen, while these allegations are pending against you, you have the right to remain silent. It's a right that's guaranteed by the United States Constitution. If anyone approaches you and wants to speak with you about these allegations, you don't have to say anything. That is your absolute constitutional right. Anything that you say to your attorney, that's private and confidential, but I have to warn you that if you do speak with other people, even friends or family, it's possible that those statements could be used against you. All right?"

THE HEARING

Hearing about my sacred right to remain silent after what I had just experienced in jail caused me to rasp out, "May I make a comment about that?"

The judge began to discourage me, pointing out that this is exactly what she was referring to. I should not talk to anyone about my case without first speaking to my lawyer. She explained that everything I said now would be on the official record.

My lawyer jumped in, "Your Honor, if I may, I think I can anticipate what Mr. Christensen was going to comment to the Court, which is it was his experience after he was arrested on Sunday by Washington County sheriff deputies that he was taken to the jail and was -- was very adamant in his exercise of his right to remain silent, and he felt that he was penalized for that by being denied access to a telephone, access to water, medication, clothing."

He continued, "Mr. Christensen had a stroke, which he was hospitalized for for three weeks in mid January, he's on four different medications, and there seems to be some complication between his desire not to speak to his jailers at all and his ability to take care of real basic needs. So I'm assuming that's what Mr. Christensen was about to comment to, but we were going to bring that up without regard."

"Is that right, Mr. Christensen?" he concluded.

"You did a better job," I affirmed.

It seemed to me the judge was a bit steamed that her soliloquy on Constitutional Rights had been made such a mockery of.

"I'm going to sign a release order," she stated.

I did not expect that. I did not expect any sympathy or breaks from the Federal legal system. My wife and I have since reflected that for all the tribulations of the stroke, it had at least kept me out of a Federal prison.

To begin the release process, I was taken to a large reception room of an office. A man with the Pretrial department had me sign a form that listed my release conditions. He sent me into a bathroom to change out of the prison jumper. I was given a too large shirt, baggy sweatpants, and bright orange tennis shoes to wear since the FBI had "lost" my suit. I was also given just one pill bottle out of my four stroke medications. I was led to an outside door at the side of the building. The sidewalk entrance way outside the door was covered with a massive steel grating with a locking gate at the end. Directly across the street was a Portland Police Department building. The windows of the police station had every window at ground level covered with plywood. Everywhere I looked, on the police building, on the plywood covering the windows, on the roads, on the sidewalks, on the street signs, was spray painted the Leftist slogan, "ACAB."

"It looks like there are a lot of people who don't like police down here," I commented to the officer leading me out to the street corner. "No one I know talks like that," I added.

My wife made good time driving in the evening traffic and she picked me up at the corner about half an hour after I was sent outside.

Thus began my entanglement with the policing arm of the Federal Government, which has been ongoing for eight months at the writing of this book, with no end yet in sight. It would lead to the recounting of a pivotal story and the realization that an ancient teaching method could bring moral truth and clarity to modern confusion.

SAVE THE KID!

Chapter 3 – The Greenhorn Protesters

It was later the same week of the arrest, as I sat up on the adjustable hospital bed that my wife had placed downstairs in the family room to facilitate my stroke recovery, that she answered a knock on our front door. It was a longtime family friend who we had not seen in over a year. She had been shopping at a store a couple of miles from our place and had decided to stop by and say hello. She had heard of my stroke at the end of January and she wanted to check in and see how we were doing.

As we chatted, she was quite surprised to learn of my encounter with the FBI. (That first week after my arrest, it was quite common for friends to laugh when they heard my incredulous story of being on the FBI's Wanted List.) As the topic turned to politics and the January 6th "Stop the Steal" rally, she told a story of the first rally she had ever attended.

It had occurred back in the year 2000 when "hanging chads" on ballots were keeping the presidential election between Bush and Gore in the news, until the Supreme Court ruled on December 12th that the recounting was over. The local Republicans decided to hold a rally to protest the interminable vote recounting.[iii] This was an activity that was totally new to suburban Republican voters. It was the first time participating in a rally for all of the people who arrived in their middle-class clothing holding their homemade signs.

The local police told the greenhorn protesters that they could wave their signs and yell at passing cars, but no one was allowed to get off the sidewalk. Our friend explained that is exactly what happened—the rally was extremely well-behaved and orderly. No one got off the sidewalk.

We all chuckled over that story. Neither my wife nor I were surprised by the Republican rally behavior. We live just ten miles from Portland Oregon, and have been well aware of the violence and destruction that had been going on by the Left for over a year in the downtown area, but well behaved, orderly, and obedient people at a Republican rally is exactly what we would have expected.

It was just a few days later that I thought of an allegory. I was still spending a lot of time sitting up in the hospital bed, and I had been writing down a lot of my thoughts, trying to make sense of the recent upheaval in our life. I am not sure what caused me to think of the allegory. I was raised going to church and had continued as an active church-goer my entire adult life, so it is not an exaggeration to say that I was taught the famous allegories, or the stories or parables, of Jesus for sixty years. I knew well that these stories were about simple aspects of everyday life, but they had such deep meaning that after 2,000 years people still discussed the spiritual truths they could reveal.

I realized with astonishment that the simple addition of a child, could change the story of the greenhorn protesters into a fictional allegory that can teach a powerful moral lesson. Here is the allegory.

> The well-behaved and proper Republican rally goers are gathered and waving their signs on a sidewalk on one side of the street. Across the street from the rally, a mother with a young

child in hand happens to meet a dear friend she has not seen in a very long time. As she excitedly talks to her friend, she doesn't notice that her child has slipped away and has wandered out into the street. A bus is coming down the street, and although it is not moving fast, it is evident from its unaltered course and speed that the driver does not see the child.

All the people at the rally see the child and understand the imminent danger. Many faces show concern, some talk about it, and a few are agitated about it. There is time to do a rescue—but *no one gets off the sidewalk*. They were told not to get off and that is the rule they obey. The child suffers a violent death. The mother turns in time to see her baby crushed to death before her eyes. No one saved the kid.

How do you see the people on the sidewalk now?

They are the same people. They haven't changed their law-abiding, obedient behavior, yet our view of them has changed instantly from admiration to repulsion. They went from being admirable moral actors to moral monsters, or at the very least moral cowards, as they did nothing to save the kid. There is something in this allegory that is important for us to understand. The next chapters will examine this more closely.

SAVE THE KID!

Chapter 4 – What Does it Mean?

One of the ongoing energetic discussions in our house, when the kids were still living at home, was about which is better, the original *Star Trek* (from my generation), or *Star Trek: The Next Generation* (from the kids' generation). My kids were always unimpressed with my cheerleading and the scifi special effects of the original show, but I hold firm to my belief that the original *Star Trek* did have some unbeatably thoughtful episodes—especially those where human morality came in contact with alien species.

One such episode I call the "Question of the Silicon Rock Creature."[iv] In the episode, we are introduced to a molten planet populated by very advanced, silicon-based life forms who scan the Enterprise and are intrigued by the human notion of good and evil. Kirk and Spock are threatened with the destruction of the Enterprise if they do not participate in a contest between good and evil so the silicon life forms can decide which is the stronger of the two.

To set up the contest, a silicon rock creature transforms a portion of his planet to earth-like conditions, creates duplicates of four of the worst evil villains from galactic history, and teams Kirk and Spock with duplicates of Abraham Lincoln and the preeminent Vulcan who inspired the Vulcan life of logic and non-violence.

Kirk, Spock, and the good guys attempt to talk and make peace, but after the murder of the famous Vulcan and of Abraham Lincoln, they use their spears and stones to fight back, engage in an all out war, and beat and scatter the enemy.

SAVE THE KID!

The silicon rock creature is totally dismayed. He says he learned nothing about the difference between good and evil. They both acted the same, they both fought and used violence to win.

This TV episode addresses the same moral question presented by our allegory. How can people who engage in the same outward behavior be labeled as moral opposites? The silicon rock creature's confusion seems justified. How can the same behavior be both good and evil?

The confusion of the silicon rock creature is cleared up by Captain Kirk. He points out that the setup of a life-or-death conflict was beyond his control. He asks the question, "What did you offer the evil side if they won?"

"What they wanted most - power, dominion, riches," the rock creature answers.

"What did you offer Spock and me if we won?"

"The lives of your crew."

This exchange teaches that it was the *motivation*, the desires of the two sides that made the difference between good and evil.

At the beginning of the allegory, the initial obedience to stay on the sidewalk was done by the rally goers due to their desire to live in an admirable, civilized society—namely one that has peace, order, the absence of contention and violence.

But later in the allegory, when they saw the danger of the child, the motivations for their obedience to stay on the sidewalk were the dark and base attributes of indecision, cowardice, and/or indifference. It would be foolish to accept the self-serving excuse of a person at the rally that staying on the sidewalk for public order outweighed the need to prevent the death of a child. The moral choice and priority here is clear and easy for anyone to see and understand.

Yet as subsequent chapters will make plain, there are many Americans who are confused and ignorant of the fact that obedience is morally agnostic. As our allegory shows, obedience can lead to either good (a peaceful rally) or evil (the death of a child). Those who obey without consideration of the context of the situation, are as morally clueless as a Silicon Rock Creature.

SAVE THE KID!

Chapter 5 – America in the Street

America has slipped its historical moorings and destructive forces are bearing down on it. To anyone who has been watching current events, the above statement is not even controversial. The demise of the world's first and greatest democratic Republic, formed "in the Name, and by Authority of the good People"* is underway.

Today American society is like people being divided into a group on the near side of the street, and another group facing them on the opposite side of the street. Our country itself, young by the standards of many established nations, is the Kid that now finds itself in the street. Rather than a bus, the destructive force heading toward the Kid is an angry mob, cheered on by a crowd on the other side of the street, enraged by the unforgivable sins and flaws they see in the Kid. This mob thunders in their collective rage, their belief that only a violent death of America's history, culture, and heritage is an acceptable remedy to these sins and flaws.

There have always been some who hated America and its Constitution, but now some among the mob are our elected leaders! They hate the sins and flaws they see in our country, and they issue edicts and pass laws that order people on the near sidewalk who love America to either stand by and do nothing to save the Kid, or worse yet, to deliver deadly blows at the Kid by engaging in unconstitutional actions that strike at its heart.

To say that the America-loving people on the sidewalk are confused and perplexed by this turn of events is an understatement. To them, the Kid, despite its flaws, has

---

* Declaration of Independence, first sentence of the last summary paragraph.

value. The Kid is something of which to be proud. It has proven to be a source of individual freedom and prosperity the like of which has never been known in the world.

Their confusion is heightened by the fact that for over 200 years the moral thing to do was relatively easy to identify in America: be an obedient citizen, be respectful to passed laws. That was the obvious way to public good. Many Americans seem ignorant of the fact that obedience to human laws can just as well lead to evil. Later chapters will demonstrate that written laws and a legal system can have nothing to do with what is morally right.*

I had a chance to see this confusion first hand when, early in 2021, I was participating in a church lesson via Zoom; the churches had been ordered closed by the Oregon state authorities because of their COVID-19 restrictions. The subject of the lesson was how to support the standards of behavior that Christ asks of us without coming off as condemning or causing contention. I thought it was a good discussion with lots of thoughtful comments from the participants.

The teacher was doing his best to guide the conversation without getting into political specifics, when at one point the chat box in the Zoom meeting lit up with some interesting words. The current discussion context made me believe that the author of the words had the January 6th Rally in mind, and he typed the phrase "we should never engage in civil disobedience."

Even though I understood the viewpoint that prompted the comment (the idea that obedience is praiseworthy), I was immediately struck by the absurdity of the phrase. I

---

* Especially covered with regard to American history in Chapter 10

immediately typed back, "What about the Founding Fathers of 1776?"

It was clear to me from the preceding discussion that most, if not all of the folks in the Zoom meeting believed that the founding of America was accomplished by the guiding hand of Providence to bring freedom to the world. What was the founding of America if not one big disobedience to civil authorities? It had rebellions against governors, the Sons of Liberty and their raging protests, the destruction of nearly $2 million dollars of tea at the Boston Tea Party, culminating with the shots fired at Lexington. All this civil disobedience was aimed at England, which was undoubtedly the authorized civil authority over the Colonies, and had been for over a hundred years.

American history surely teaches the folly of "obedience is always good." Yet a member of the group had just intoned that civil authorities should always be obeyed.

It made me realize that the question of obedience is a more complex topic than many people realize. Even the Founding Fathers of America themselves wrestled with the question of obedience and its relationship to governments and citizens. The next Section shows why, as the historical good, bad, and ugly of obedience will be discussed.

II. Outcomes of Obedience

SAVE THE KID!

Chapter 6 – The Good

Every society depends on the majority of its citizens to obey the strictures and culture of the land. If malevolent tyranny or insatiable greed corrupts the leadership of the land, the norms of obedience fade away and eventually total collapse occurs as the culture becomes inimical to the interests of the people. But when the rules of a society are beneficial to people—and the people understand and voluntarily obey the rules—the benefits can be enormous.

One of the stories I grew up with was of the city of Nauvoo, Illinois.[v] In the 1830s and 1840s the city was bigger than Chicago. It was on the edge of the American frontier along the Mississippi River, but instead of the rough characters and rough buildings usually found on the frontier, it had large wide streets, with red brick homes and businesses on large lots. The inhabitants were religious refugees who originally came to a swamp land no one else wanted. To found their town, they cooperated in a massive project to drain a nearly 800 acre swamp, digging a canal eight feet deep and eleven feet across for nearly three-quarters of a mile.[vi] They were families who not only went to church, but had raised on the edge of the wilderness a magnificent multi-story white-stone worship building 160 feet tall, which they called the Nauvoo Temple.

Many people who came to the city, especially civic leaders, would marvel at what they saw. Once a member of the State Legislature came and saw the effective governance and perfect order, and asked how it was possible. Their religious leader simply replied, "I teach them correct principles, and they govern themselves."[vii]

That statement has always stuck in my mind as it seems to me a perfect synopsis of the American spirit of government. I think it is exactly this sentiment that John Adams expressed when he said that the government set up by the Constitution "was made only for a moral and religious People. It is wholly inadequate to the government of any other."[viii]

Why wouldn't the majority of people be supportive of and obedient to a way of life that respected them as individuals, gave them space to be themselves, gave them freedom and protection from power-crazed tyrants, and protected them from those who would steal the labor of their own hands?

On the other hand, it is also self-evident a society that slides more and more toward heavy-handed legal enforcement, proliferation of officers and jails, and the domination of lawyers and judges, is a society that is moving away from the American ideal.

I have heard orderly societies like Nauvoo be called "Trust Societies."[ix] You can see a Trust Society in operation every day in America, including in the Willamette Valley of Oregon where we have lived for over 30 years. During that time, I had dealings with many contractors and suppliers where the transaction of deals and agreement to terms was only done verbally. Often, the only piece of paper was an invoice that listed the agreed upon cost of the deal.

What amazing efficiency and productivity such a system provides! If obedience to promises and contracts was *not* the normal behavior of people, if we lived in a country where nothing but expensive legal documents, lawyers, police, fines, and jail would induce anyone to keep a bargain, the wheels of development would grind to a crawl under the weight of the extra baggage.

Americans recognized the advantages of self-imposed civic obedience in their new Constitutional Republic. They created a Trust Society that carved out of the wilderness, in a short time, the most powerful and prosperous nation the world has ever seen.

But we will see that the story of obedience does not *always* lead to such a result.

SAVE THE KID!

Chapter 7 – The Bad

One of the realizations that I have made from a lifetime interest in reading about history, is to notice that all the cultures and nations of the earth seem to have something in common: they all have a word that identifies the top ruler—the king, the pharaoh, the emperor, the sultan, the caesar.

Except for some early attempts at democracy among the Greeks and the Romans, is there any culture in extant history that grew from tribal leadership to anything other than leadership by a single powerful individual? Anywhere you look, from Asia, to India, to Africa, to Europe, for 5,000 years of recorded history, you find that everyone was familiar with the concept of a king.

And all these kingdoms were able to successfully operate in their turn because the members of those societies were obedient to their rules. One of the earliest examples of the rules of a kingdom is the Code of Hammurabi, which is dated to around 1750 BC. The code was found on a seven-foot basalt stele that has over 4,000 lines of cuneiform text carved into it. The code lists criminal law, family law, property law, and commercial law. [x]

The prologue of the Code makes clear the source of authority for these laws is from the Babylonian sun god and god of justice, who gave these rules directly to King Hammurabi. The concept of the "divine right of kings" is an ancient concept that continues to the present day in some areas of the world.

The members of this kingdom were enjoined by all that was holy to obey these laws—but were these laws enacted with a universal justice in mind? Certainly not. The Code of Hammurabi lists laws that are applicable to slaves, so obviously that society accepted that some people could be enslaved[xi]—that, in and of itself, contradicts the possibility of universal justice. Plus, this code had rules for nobles and those for commoners.[xii] Seeing that division of rules confirms my reading of history that one of the key purposes of the "divine right of kings" concept, and the laws that came from it, was to perpetuate the rule of the small noble class over the mass of the people.

It is true the rule of kings allowed complex societies to arise. Kingdoms provided a way for rules and order to be developed so large groups of people could live together and cooperate, so in that sense, there certainly was some advantage to everyone who lived in a kingdom.

However, there is a definite downside to a society arranged with "kings, nobles, commoners, and slaves." This downside was emphasized to me one day as I watched a YouTube clip dealing with economics. The narrator said something jarring while showing a graph of the total economic output of the world over time.[xiii] The graph was basically a line that hugged the bottom axis near zero until the year marked 1700, at which time it started an almost vertical climb to the top. The narrator in explaining the graph said, "around 1700, democracies appeared."

It was incredulous to me the way the narrator totally glossed over the six years of brutal warfare[xiv] that Americans waged (and mostly lost) in their nearly failed struggle to become the world's first democracy. But I was intrigued by the economic graph of the world's wealth shown on the screen. What was it about democracy that caused the exponential rise of human wealth and financial well being? The video clip did not address that question. But if you know anything about king societies you will know another key purpose of the "divine right of kings"—to keep the king rich.

Abraham Lincoln, in a speech replying to his opponent during the contest for a senate seat in Illinois in 1858[xv], called out this point when he said that the attitude of nobles and the attitude of slave-holders is the same. Both hold the view that society has those whose "right it is to ride" and those whose fate "it is to be ridden." He further noted the phony *noblesse oblige* where these rulers would virtuously explain that they didn't want to be rich tyrants, but it was their duty to provide order and leadership "and that people were better off for being ridden." And it was the proper order of things to say, "you work, and I eat."

The main reason for poverty in the world as shown in the graph is the rulers of the world spent the first 5,000 years of recorded human history using their power to steal whatever they wanted from those who produced it. The vast majority of people were left to be dirt poor so a small number of rulers could build fantastic palaces and thrones—and wage constant wars among themselves for even more dominance and control.

The appearance of the American idea, that political power is of the people, by the people, and for the people was as unique and enlightening to the human experience as a supernova is to space. For the first time, citizens of a country had some protection from the rapaciousness of rulers and their governments of suppression and theft, and had the motivation to prosper as their own industry allowed.

Is it any coincidence that so much of the innovation of the industrial revolution occurred here, in America, where a person was better enabled to rise to their full potential, independent of their class at birth? And is it any wonder that laws allowing human enslavement were eventually exorcised as antithetical to this American idea?

The successful founding of America and its rise to preeminence and prosperity opened the door to people throughout the world to embrace its enlightened concept of democracy. This shift allowed millions of individuals to grasp their own potential, prosperity, and freedom, by curtailing the power of governments over them.

The American way replaced an obedience to the "divine right of kings" that had caused widespread despotism and poverty for millennia. Yet as will be shown next, things can get even worse than they were when mankind was under the rule of kings. Let us now examine what can become the "ugly" of obedience.

Chapter 8 – The Ugly

A mother in our church congregation once commented that she feels really old when her young kids erroneously say she was from the "19th century" because she was born in the 1980s.

While young kids may see prior years as ages ago, to me, a "boomer" who was raised by parents who lived through World War II, the ugliness of those horrible decades does not seem far away. From a very young age, I was always consuming books about those war years. As an avid student of military history, it was of intense interest to me, when in my twenties, I was able to visit Germany.

This visit was possible because I had signed up for Army ROTC for the last years of working on my undergraduate degree in Electrical Engineering which I completed in 1983. I had married Myra in July 1979 after I had just turned twenty-one, immediately after getting back from two years of missionary service in South Korea. We had our first son in 1980 and our second in 1982 while we both were attending school. After college I received a Second Lieutenant's commission and an active duty assignment. We packed up the family to head to officer basic school in Georgia, and then to our first post—a four year tour to Germany. It was the summer of 1983 when I went on active duty, during the years when President Reagan was rebuilding the US Military after the malaise years following the Vietnam War.

My first unit was First of the Sixth Mechanized Infantry Battalion in southeastern Germany, part of the 1st Armored Division, in the sector of VIIth Corps near the Czechoslovakian border. Our battalion's task was to slow the onslaught of Soviet tanks by thirty minutes before we were annihilated. In later years, while working on microprocessor design teams at Intel, I would tell new engineers out of school that my first job was "being a Russian speed bump."

At the time of the move to Germany, my wife was seven months pregnant with our third son, and the regular military procedure of sending the soldier ahead of the family and then bringing the family over six months later was not appealing. As an officer, I signed a paper refusing Army housing and took responsibility to find my own housing nearby in the local German community. This turned out to be a great outcome, as we always loved living in local towns among the German people during our stay in the country.

Our first house was in Bad Windsheim, the next town over from where the Army post was located. The woman who ran the guest house where we first stayed had found for us a triangle-shaped house for rent on a winding street near the center of the 700-year-old town. As we initially had only one car, my wife learned to navigate the local town on foot. Fortunately for her travels, the downtown shops were just around the corner and within walking distance. However, we learned that the American-style folding baby stroller with four inch wheels would rattle the baby and shake apart on the cobblestone streets of the city, so we obtained a good old style perambulator—one like a British nanny would use for a walk in the park. The wheels were a good 8-10 inches in diameter and it had a sturdy metal spring-suspension system.

My wife often shared with me what happened to her when she would walk through town with a baby and a toddler in the perambulator, with a third little boy holding on to the handle. Almost without fail, older German ladies, women

THE UGLY

who would be of grandma age, would come streaming out of their houses to gather around the perambulator to admire and interact with the *buben* (little boys).

It took us a while to understand this was because most of these older women had no grandchildren of their own. Even by the 1980s, the marriage and birth rate in Germany had cratered, and there were precious few children to be seen.

But it was the behavior of these German ladies and many other such experiences that taught me a valuable lesson—*the German people are just good, normal people.* Despite the wartime propaganda of the "evil Hun", there is nothing wrong or inherently sinister about their character that would make them uniquely susceptible to the vile dogma of Hitler and the National Socialist German Workers' Party (aka the Nazi Party).

So what was it that allowed their country to be dragged down into the gutter of vicious tyranny, devastating expansionist war, and murderous genocide? At the top of the list, I would put obedience. The German people had many troubles during and after World War I, but remember—they had become a united, advanced, and a very successful society before that point. As we have seen, this only happens when the people are united around a culture and a set of rules that are almost universally accepted and obeyed.

Many people forget that Hitler and his followers had a socialist political party in the elections that ran on a platform promising to eliminate the tribulations of the people through government control and regulation. This party had great success with that message amidst the troubles after the Great

War. Through his party's success, Hitler became the chosen Chancellor in an open election before he maneuvered himself to become Supreme Ruler, or Fuhrer.[xvi] In the eyes of the German people, Hitler had obtained political legitimacy through the voice of the people—he had obtained the legal authority to be obeyed.

One of the infamous phrases that arose in the aftermath of the terrible decades of the National Socialist years in Germany, is "I was just obeying orders." This seemed to be the line that everyone involved in atrocities and barbarity used to try to rationalize their obedience. During the Nuremberg war crime trials after the war, one of the German defendants did a good job of summarizing this mindset, "You simply can't refuse to obey a military order. That is a perfectly absurd idea. That isn't done in the army."[xvii]

That's not what I learned in the Army. When I was in the American Army in the 1980s, it was drilled into my head over and over to honor the commissioning oath to "uphold and defend the Constitution of the United States," and to only obey "Constitutional orders." This meant you were expected to refuse or even actively resist orders not in harmony with the Constitution. This mantra was repeated endlessly by an Army Chain of Command that had just been traumatized by instances of out-of-control leaders and obedient soldiers who had committed war crimes in the recent war in Vietnam[xviii]— and by Army leaders who presumably were still freshly aware of what happens to a country when people mindlessly say *Sieg Heil* to orders.

The other big "ugly" of obedience that was a constant fixture of my growing up years were the communists around the world, and especially in the Soviet Union. They were the reason I was in the Army and was sent to Germany to be a speed bump.

For any person willing to look during those years, there was too much information disclosing the atrocities committed by communists to believe these tyrants were doing it "for the people." The starvation of Ukraine and the gulags of Stalin with its 20 million dead were being disclosed by books from Soviet dissidents, such as Alexander Solzhenitsyn.[xix] I read those books and many others, like the account of Victor Belenko, the Mig-25 pilot who defected by flying his plane to Japan.[xx]

As a preteenager, I paid more attention than most youth to the Vietnam War as my Dad was an Air Force pilot who was sent overseas to the war. My parents ended up sponsoring a Vietnamese boy who had fled to the open sea to escape the communist purges after the fall. Those communist horrors were well known to me.

Oh my goodness, speaking of Asia! Words cannot even begin to catalog the evil that the communists have perpetrated on that continent: tens of millions who suffered the cruel fate of starvation at the hands of Mao,[xxi] the Cambodian people who saw one in four of their countrymen mercilessly murdered in the name of equality,[xxii] and the people enduring the ongoing cruel abomination of the North Korean regime.

A thought that continually occurred to me as I witnessed during my lifetime the ongoing parade of ugly horrors of the communists around the world was, how can this happen? Many of the writers of the time would say it happened because "Stalin sent millions to the gulag," and it happened because "Mao took food from starving Chinese to send to Eastern Europe." But these statements are nothing more than the third-cousin of a half-truth. Those tyrants surely gave the orders, but what about the thousands, tens of thousands, or even millions of people who decided to obey those orders? What about the police forces who rounded up their fellow citizens, the prison guards who sadistically tortured their inmates, the truck drivers and train engineers who delivered prisoners, the snitches working for the government who turned people in, and all the people who decided to say and do nothing against it?

No, this amount of evil is not done by one person; it takes an obedient *village*.

One would think after such monumental evil of the Nazis and Communists in the 20th century that every human soul would be stamped with an indelible warning of the ugly that can come from wrongful obedience.

Yet, as the next chapter frighteningly reveals, the "ugly" of obedience has surfaced again—and this time, it is right here at home.

Chapter 9 - The Ugly Comes Home

After the horrific years of genocide and barbarism of the Second World War, a good and righteous saying arose: "Never Again." It was a statement of determination from good people to learn from the evils just perpetrated and to do whatever was necessary to prevent them from ever happening again.

A lesson from that saying that *should* have been cemented in people's minds is if someone, no matter his or her position of civic authority, orders you to do something evil, *you don't do it*. Does that take some moral courage? Sure it does. If the path of least resistance is all you're interested in, being a spineless moral coward is always the choice you want.

So did the world learn its lesson? Have we all embraced "Never Again" in our hearts in order to avoid reliving the horror of the last century? Below are a couple of personal stories just from within the last few of months. Judging from the ease at which I came across these stories, it's undoubtedly true Americans could tell thousands or even tens of thousands of stories that indicate we have not learned the lessons we should have, and that the ugly side of obedience has come to our country.

After my arrest and prosecution by the FBI for participating in the January 6th Stop the Steal rally in Washington DC, I had been doing some speaking engagements to talk about the state of our country and the rule of law by the Constitution. At one of these events I met a young woman, who I will call Susan, who came up to tell me her story.

SAVE THE KID!

Susan is a woman in her 30s of Asian heritage. She indicated she too had gone to Washington DC to participate in the Stop the Steal rally. She was one of the 100,000s of folks who did not approach the steps or enter the Capitol Building; she simply walked around outside on the National Mall. Imagine her surprise when a crowd of FBI agents showed up at her house and proceeded to aggressively interrogate her and her husband about what she was doing there, what she was wearing, what she was carrying, etc. Finally her husband, in total exasperation, cried out, "What are you people doing? She peacefully participated in a protest...in America!"

At that one of the FBI agents replied, "I'm just doing my job."

This story fills me with sadness—for a couple different reasons. First, Susan told me that she was of Indonesian heritage, and that many years ago she immigrated to America, brimming with brightness and hope at the privilege of coming to the shining land of the free. As she told this story, she made it clear to me that her feeling of being uniquely free was now gone. Getting the political third degree from government agents was not something this American newcomer at all expected.

Another angle of sadness comes from hearing an American FBI agent engaged in political persecution echo the words that came from the Nuremberg Trials[xxiii]. Can anyone please explain to me the difference between the phrases, "I'm just doing my job" and "I'm just following orders"? The storied and honorable FBI is being converted into an American version of the KGB, the secret police force of the former Soviet communists, and your response to orders of political persecution is "I'm just doing my job"?!

Another experience caused me to make a frightening comparison to something I had read in the book ***Ordinary Men.***[xxiv] The book is a story of a police reserve battalion from the city of Berlin during the Second World War. The battalion was made up of middle aged family men who were activated and sent to Poland to participate in the rounding up of the Jewish population. The book documents how these men, who anyone would classify as respectable policemen, were turned into ruthless killers who ended up directly committing mass murder of men, women, and children. At the morning formation of their very first roundup operation, the battalion commander asked that anyone who had misgivings should step forward, as they would be excused.[xxv]

Compare that to the story directly told to me by a National Guard staff sergeant in my home state of Oregon. Governor Kate Brown decided during the summer of 2021 that every healthcare worker in the State, public or private, who did not obey her order to get a COVID vaccine, would be fired.[xxvi] [xxvii] In the wisdom that can only come from a government bureaucracy, the State realized that firing hundreds or thousands of nurses and doctors from an industry that is always short of help might be a problem—so they would activate the National Guard![xxviii] Did they think the National Guard had thousands of doctors, ICU nurses, pediatric specialists, etc., to seamlessly fill those spots?

The staff sergeant I talked to was an Engineer, a term in the Army that means he had learned to blow up structures of the enemy and how to build things our side needed. He was appalled when he was told that he was being activated not to do the job he was trained to do, but so the State could fire healthcare workers, whose unforgivable crime was they wanted to make their own risk decisions on their health.

SAVE THE KID!

This was an earth-shaking event for him. He thought about his oath to uphold the Constitution and realized that this would be helping the government impose servitude over the people. He thoughtfully wrote up a four page document that expressed the Constitutional violations of this action and asked to be excused.

This fight is ongoing, but it is not going well for him. So far, his chain of command is treating him as an insubordinate agitator who is way out of line. He does not know if he faces punishment or a dishonorable discharge. He told me that he should have known better than to sign up for another six-year commitment when, a few months before this activation order, he was sent to a mandatory briefing where the soldiers were told that the Constitution does not apply to Americans in the military. They are always required to obey orders and to not question or complain.

What a contrast to the military of my younger years thirty years earlier, which honored the Constitution and expected soldiers to use it to guide their conscience and their actions!

So here we have a comparison that should leave every American with a sickening sense of dread: the decision to opt out of an order due to individual conscience is given more respect by leaders of a German police battalion engaging in gruesome genocide than is given by leaders in the chain of command of an American citizen soldier.

As these recent experiences show, the ugly side of obedience, where people, in order to avoid "trouble," jettison their free will and courage, and where they choose to become soulless puppets obediently helping to perpetrate evil, has fully arrived in America.

In this section of the book we have seen how obedience to laws and orders can lead to good, bad, or ugly outcomes. In the next section, we will learn how to judge the things to which we give our obedience so we can follow a path that leads to good.

SAVE THE KID!

III. Using an Inner Moral Compass

SAVE THE KID!

Chapter 10 - Be Law-Abiding, Right?

Here in America, we have representatives that produce laws, police enforcement, and courts and judges for protection, so we may think it wouldn't be possible for a law-abiding citizen to perpetrate evil while also obeying the law.

However, all of the societies of the 20th century that committed crimes against humanity on the scale of tens of millions also had laws and legal systems. Most of them even had a representative body—albeit, occupied by puppets and yes-men (is that so unlike many of the current representatives in our country?). Having a solemn official set of laws or even a legislature is not an indicator of a society that adheres to what is moral and right.

More often than not, America has been true to its Constitutional charter in the past—besides some local and state laws that were immoral outliers. However, there have been times when things have, *nationally,* gone wrong in a major way. One of the most infamous cases occurred right before the Civil War and involved an enslaved black man named Dred Scott.[xxix] He had been taken to a free state and a free territory, and he filed a suit with the contention that he should be set free.

After seven years of legal fighting, the US Supreme Court finally ruled that Mr. Scott did not have the right to sue in the first place, because no person of African descent could become a citizen of the United States, and therefore no person of African descent could sue. The Court further ruled that Congress had no power to forbid or abolish slavery in the territories! A southern newspaper later crowed, "the

Southern opinion on the subject of Southern slavery is now the supreme law of the land."[xxx]

Many Northern States ignored the atrocious ruling and passed laws that would automatically free any enslaved people brought into their state. Many individuals continued to oppose slavery even more vehemently, including running the Underground Railroad to smuggle fugitives from the South up into Canada.

Regardless of what the Court said with its legal reasoning and its twisting and wrangling of the Constitution, the moral question here is an easy one to answer. If the law ordered you to turn over a fugitive on the Underground Railroad and return him to his pursuers for certain punishment, torture, and further enslavement, the answer must be no.

This example of rejecting legal immorality is not a hard one to decide. In that sense, it is much like the allegory of the Kid in the street. It should be easy to see that acting in a way that facilitates the death of the American Republic is not a moral act, even if the action is what the law dictates you "should" do.

In later chapters, examples from our current time that are causing moral confusion to Americans will be discussed. For now, it should be clear from this historical example, that just because something is a law, even if ratified by judicial bodies, that does not make it moral. Something else besides the law is needed so one can be guided on how to be a moral actor.

Chapter 11 – The Need for a Compass

Things are starting to look pretty bleak in the moral landscape. Words and actions that are often used as markers of moral character, such as "obedience" and "law-abiding," have been shown to be useless for marking a path that guides between right and wrong. Some other moral guide is clearly needed.

As part of my completion of ROTC back in college, I attended a summer camp for training cadets held in Fort Lewis, Washington. Part of officer training back then, before the days of GPS and electronic maps, was to learn the use of a paper map and a compass. This had been part of many ROTC classes and field trips, so I was familiar enough with it to totally empathize with Daniel Boone when he replied, "I can't say as ever I was lost, but I was bewildered once for three days."[xxxi]

On one of the training days at camp, a mix-up by our bus driver brought us to a compass course long after the timed event had begun. Our group still needed to keep the schedule for the rest of the day, so our time to complete the course was limited. My course partner and I decided that the only way to complete in time was to avoid walking a long loop on dirt roads and trails, and to cut directly across a heavily forested area.

In the Pacific Northwest, on the west side of the Cascade Mountain range where Fort Lewis is located, a description of "heavily forested" is an understatement. The mountains block the prevailing westerly winds that come from the ocean, and the area receives on average 48 inches of rain a year that can be continuous for nine months. These "temperate rain forests" can rival the more familiar denseness of a tropical rain forest. During one outing at camp, I remember encountering a lush field of ferns that towered over my head, and thought I wouldn't have been too surprised to see a dinosaur reaching down to munch on them.

So we pulled out the map, took a compass bearing across the forest that would lead us just to the east of the next waypoint, and proceeded to bush crash. The only way the shortcut would work was to be perfectly on course. Even a small variation across the long distance would cause us to be uncertain about the location of the waypoint and to waste time searching for it. Many times we were on hands and knees getting through dense vegetation in order to keep a perfectly straight path.

And it worked! Our course completion time was top notch, and my confidence in using a compass was greatly increased. Later, as a new Second Lieutenant in the Army, I never had the problem of being "bewildered" about my location.

From this experience, an analogy can be made that the solution to navigating the dense forests of life, which obscure the morally straight path, is to *use a compass*! Each person on the course of life needs to make constant use of an internal moral compass. The next chapters will reveal what can be used as a moral compass and how it can be used.

The main moral problem in American politics today is people are confused about what to use as a guide. Most people have an inherent understanding of right and wrong, but they cannot seem to find the true path between them. Their problem is in their use of a compass.

Chapter 12 – Finding the Right Compass

A religious person is totally familiar with the concept of an internal moral compass. The main point of a spiritual life is to acknowledge a higher power for truth that exists outside of the worldly constructs of men, and that God has eternally defined what is good and right. This true morality is usually not aligned with human legal constructs, and is most definitely *not* a social construct of the current time, and is not up for debate. A dedicated religious disciple can spend a lifetime improving his obedience to the higher laws of Heaven.

Yet despite the blessing of having a solid spiritual moral compass in the Western world based on Judeo-Christian teachings, the traditional religion of the West is a moral compass not directly concerned with politics.

This was a difficult concept for the early Jewish people who followed Christ as the Messiah. Jesus taught that he came to earth to establish the Kingdom of Heaven. He was not here to help the Jews overcome the political oppression of Rome, but to bring the grace for individual salvation by overcoming sin with repentance. Jesus beautifully summarized this in the famous phrase,

> *Render therefore unto Caesar*
> *the things that be Caesar's,*
> *and unto God the things which be God's.* *

It should be remembered that the early Christian church grew and spread widely in the Roman political system (which was, at this later point of their history, a dictatorial empire that

---

* Luke 20:25 King James version of the Bible

embraced slavery in a big way). Such growth indicates that much of the time, Christians—who were attempting to follow their inner spiritual compass—were not continually hunted for extermination. Rather, they only suffered martyrdom during distinct periods of intense persecution.

Roman records indicate that civic leaders recognized the moral teachings of Christianity actually created good citizens, but that Christians were at odds with the religion of the Empire.[xxxii] Starting with a ruling from Emperor Trajan, throughout the second century and part of the third, it was imperial policy not to seek out Christians for persecution, but still to punish them when they were brought before the authorities.[xxxiii]

Thus the most common pitfall for early Christians was getting involved with the legal system and courts of Rome. Those courts required an oath to the Roman pantheon of gods, much like the truthfulness oaths of American courts on the Bible. These oaths included an acknowledgment that the Emperor was a god on earth.[xxxiv] That was a big problem for Christians who were determined to follow their spiritual moral compass that there is only one God—and that one God was definitely not the often reprehensible guy on the throne of Rome. A legal case was a deadly danger, since a contempt of court charge back then was swiftly punished at the end of a sword.

Today in America, religious individuals and leaders get involved in politics due to moral issues as local, state, and federal governments stray further away from the Judeo-Christian roots of the American Founding. Yet many of the hot political issues of the day—like mask directives, quarantine lockdowns, and government-enforced vaccine mandates—are often viewed as issues belonging to Caesar and do not register on that moral compass.

However, there is a moral compass that is constantly and openly applied to politics in America. It is strongly held by a large segment of the population and is commonly used to guide people to disregard the law. The moral compass in mind is that which belongs to the political Left.

If that statement seems jarring to you, it shouldn't be. The evidence for the existence of the inner moral compass of the Left is irrefutable. I was born in 1958, and I was old enough to observe the world of the late 1960s. Ever since that time, the American Left has engaged in "protests" that have proven the existence of its moral compass. The law breaking and violence of those events are always excused with the claim they are being done in the service of a higher cause.[xxxv]

As noted in the story of the Greenhorn protesters and the allegory of the Kid, the American Right is a latecomer to the political protest. And to this day, the Right has no idea what makes a "successful" protest. The point of a protest is not to "make your voices heard," especially not in the literal way conservatives take that statement—to mean you wave signs, give speeches, chant, and cheer. That is not a protest; it is a rally. People making noise on the street is not where political power comes from in America. Real political power comes from the election system, and a politician has nothing to fear from a rally on the street—even if they are noisy.

No, the success of the Left in continually assaulting and dismantling American traditions, heritage, and history for my entire lifetime is due to their knowledge that a successful protest causes *trouble*.

A rally on the street has very little to no effect on a politician, but a small group causing trouble is an entirely different matter. For years the *trouble* aspect of a Democrat protest consisted of things like occupying buildings, blocking roads, and some battling of police. However, the Black Lives Matter protests of 2020 saw the Left add arson, destruction of property, and assault to the list of acceptable trouble from a protest.

No constituency likes to see trouble in their community, so a politician will quickly cave in response to it. The easiest and most expedient thing for a politician to do is to quickly meet the demands of the protesters and to send some money their way.

And by the way, the work of Martin Luther King Jr. and the Civil Rights protests of the 1960s[xxxvi] were most assuredly *not* a success belonging to the Left. It was an *American* success, because it turned America closer to a truth of its founding that all men are created equal. The moral compass that guided the "trouble" of civil disobedience by Dr. King and so many Americans of all political persuasions, was the religious moral compass that says all men are created equal before God—no matter what the laws of the state said. (Remember Dr. King was a *reverend* and spoke constantly of the spiritual aspects of the struggle.)

By way of contrast, the BLM protests of 2020 were a success of the Left. They condemned the entire concept of America, led to increased racial animosity, and violated the rights and safety of fellow citizens—not to mention the destruction of life, property, and order that should be a hallmark of a civil

FINDING THE RIGHT COMPASS

society. And true to tradition, the politicians caved and bowed to the demands of these protests.

Any human being who is not a psychopath will realize that destroying the civilization and culture by dismantling the laws and order, which provide your living environment, is a dangerous thing to do. So how can so many people support it? The answer is they respond to an inner moral compass that they see taking precedence over the laws and customs of society. What the Right sees as "barbarians at the gates," the Left sees as righteous and superior moral actors.

It can be challenging to identify the moral compass of the Left, because their tactic *du jour* is constantly changing. However, whether the reason for their current condemnation of America is due to financial inequity, immigration, racism, homelessness, same-sex attraction, or cross-sex dysphoria, the thing these condemnations all have in common is their root in the goal of the Left to create a socialist utopia.

Yes, a vision of a socialist utopia is the inner moral compass of the Left. This is the reason why no amount of American progress or improvement in society will ever be enough. America, as it was founded, can never measure up to this imagined perfection, so the Left's morality dictates that America itself must be removed. Paraphrasing what was so infamously said of Stalin, if a few eggs (or heads) need to be cracked to cook the omelet of utopia, it is surely worth the price.[xxxvii]

What about those on the Right who have a positive view of America?

Can a person who understands and loves the amazing promise of individual freedom of the American Founding have an inner compass that provides moral political guidance? Many on the Right are religious disciples who spend their life working on consistent obedience to the moral compass of God's laws. Should this same attitude of respectful obedience also apply to the laws of men? Are those on the Right, as caricatured by zealots of the Left, doomed to be soulless political automatons, obedient to all government laws or orders, whether good or evil, which might appear?

What is the political moral compass for the Right, if not the law? The answer is so obvious it is astounding so few Americans are making use of it—the political inner moral Compass for the patriot are the principles of the United States Constitution.

IV. The Constitution as Compass

SAVE THE KID!

Chapter 13 - Principles of Freedom

Are there hallowed principles of freedom in the Constitution of the United States that make it the perfect political moral Compass for the American patriot?

The answer is yes, but sadly there are entire swaths of the American "elite" in politics, media, education, entertainment, and so on who condemn the American Founding and the Constitution. Even more disturbing is the trashing of the Constitution which is now commonly done by judges who ignore plain sentences or invent ideas not written in the text in order to nullify its principles. This animosity is a new development in our history.

Our ancestors who set up the American system understood the majesty of the Constitution. They universally decided that every office holder, every public servant, every military person, and every new citizen should take an oath to support and defend the Constitution.

Some of the amazing political principles of the Constitution will be examined in this chapter, in order to bolster the belief of the citizen in the morality of the Constitution and its fitness for the role of Compass in the face of these attacks on its integrity.

Voice of the People

The concept that the voice of the people is the source of political legitimacy, as expressed in open elections, could be termed the heart of the Constitution. Today this concept is so widely accepted throughout every corner of the world, one can seriously ask the question if there exists a person who does not believe it.

Yet as discussed in a previous chapter, the "divine right of kings," the "mandate of Heaven," or simply the use of war and brute force were the vast majority of the accepted means of instituting government authority for most of mankind before the late 1700s.

The bedrock upon which this principle of universal suffrage is built is the truth described in the Declaration of Independence, that all men are created equal and are endowed with unalienable rights from God. The American Founding utterly rejects the idea that there is a class of people with special rights to rule. Instead, each person has the right to use free will to choose government leaders from among his equals. These leaders are to be servants to the people, not the other way around.

Separation of Powers

Each Colony retained its own government when it joined the *United States* of America. These states joined a *federal* government, as defined by the dictionary, "pertaining to a league or treaty; derived from an agreement or covenant between parties."[xxxviii]

It was determined the States would retain their identity and sovereignty over local things, and would band together to form a national government that had sovereignty over things best done by a central power. Splitting functions between Federal and independent State governments in this way is quite different from other countries such as France, where provinces are simply organizational departments within the monolithic national government.

This same "separation of powers" concept is seen in the formation of the Federal government, in the system of checks and balances enumerated between the legislative, executive, and judicial branches. Each branch is given specific governing duties and powers designed to keep the other branches from accumulating power and gaining ascendancy.

The separation of powers found throughout the Constitution addresses the concerns of the Founders about the danger of a concentrated government arising from the faulty tendency of almost all men who are placed in authority to grope after even more power.

Limitation of Powers

The English Magna Carta and the existence of Parliament were notable outliers in the world at the time of the American Founding, when governments of kings and rulers assumed they had unlimited power to make law on any subject.

The Constitution limits the power of government by specifically listing the items to be handled by a central government, and by the state governments. The remainder of powers not listed are retained by the people. In other words, the Constitution was written to put a strict limit on what the government should be doing.

It was for this reason some of the Founders were not enthusiastic about including the Bill of Rights as the first ten amendments to the Constitution. They were worried that listing the rights of the people would water down the granting of all unspecified rights to the people, and the Bill of Rights would imply these rights were the only ones the people had.

Freedom of Thought

One thing I found interesting during our stay in Germany during the 1980s was how areas of the country each had a different dominant religion. The historical churches or cathedrals in a certain area were all Catholic or all Lutheran, depending on where you were.

This pattern is due to the horrendous wars over religion in Europe starting in the early part of the 16th century.[xxxix] These wars devastated Germany and killed one-third of its population! The seeds for conflict began when various Protestant sects arose; due to widespread printing and translation of the Bible, a growing knowledge of history and doctrine of the scriptures, and to "protest" against practices seen in the medieval Catholic church—such as the selling of "indulgences" to grant forgiveness of sins by payment of money.

The people of Europe, and especially the rulers, decided it was impossible that a single nation or political entity could effectively have more than one religious belief within its borders. This is an idea a modern person with tepid or non-existent religious beliefs simply cannot understand, but to medieval people, church was not just about what building you attended for worship, or what religious clothes you might wear. Religion formed one's central philosophy and thoughts about everything that mattered in life.

With that in mind, the kings and rulers in Europe proceeded to force everyone in their kingdom to believe the same as they did. It turns out people did not take kindly to this tyranny over their deeply held religious beliefs. For over 200 years, neighbor fought against neighbor, town against town, until the entire continent was ravaged and destroyed—but finally, after *centuries* of conflict, everyone could sit down on their rocker on their burned out porch and sigh in relief that all their few remaining maimed neighbors in their charred and rubble strewn town had the same religious thoughts as they did.

The American Founders had a different idea. They called it the right to Freedom of Religion, but more descriptively it could be called the right to Freedom of Thought.

In America, you are free to decide on the things that matter in life, and you are free to decide how you should live to be in harmony with those ideals. Your neighbor has the same privilege you do. All that is required for a civil society is to respect each other as outlined in the Constitution—to preserve each others freedoms of speech, assembly, property rights, religion, and so on. You do not have the right to attack others' beliefs as hate, to claim your viewpoint alone is allowable, or to use the power of the state to force someone else to convert to your beliefs. To do so is to return to the narrow-minded and evil practices of the tyrannical European nobles.

The Protection of Diversity

For all the constant yammering about *diversity* from America disparaging people on the Left (which strangely leads them to the conclusion of enforced uniformity), the first Americans who took concrete steps to ensure diversity were the Founders. They did this not only through the previously mentioned Freedom of Thought, but by apportioning political power in the Constitution to protect the minority.

America does *not* have a "one man one vote" political system. The potentially fatal flaw of such a system is 51 percent of the voters could vote the other 49 percent should be enslaved. From a historical perspective, the Founders were well aware of the trouble that contributed to the downfall of freedom in Rome when political leaders began to wield power by providing "bread and circuses"[xl] to win the large number of votes of the masses of the city.

To solve this problem, the Founders reached what is called the "Grand Compromise."[xli] This solution, composed of the idea that each Colony, big or small, would get two senators in Congress, allowed the Colonies to agree on the Constitution. While it is often written about as simply a political compromise, it has a tremendous beneficial moral effect. Transferring some political power to the more rural areas, and away from the dense populations, helps prevent the States with large populations from overwhelming the wishes of the States with smaller populations.

One can see other applications of this principle of "location representation" in the Constitution. For instance, in the Electoral College, which uses the States' numbers of representatives and senators as the election count. The weight of the populous States in picking the President is muted, so a more expansive appeal to other States is required to win.

One of the mindless phrases that I heard in my American civic classes and is often repeated, is "the Founders did not trust the majority." When I hear that statement I wonder why someone is using two negatives to create a hostile, disparaging, plausibly logical conversion of a positive goal in the Constitution. The goal the Founders had in mind was to protect diversity and the rights of the minority.

This listing of some of the amazing principles of freedom of the Constitution reminds us of why it is such a precious document and how it gave rise to the strength and prosperity of America in such a short period of time. One of the truths of life that I have gained from reading history is whenever people are relieved of tyranny and given the freedom to pursue supporting themselves and their family without theft and strangulating restrictions, prosperity will surely follow.

The United States Constitution is a worthy document to be used as a Compass that shows a moral political path.

SAVE THE KID!

Chapter 14 – Reading the Compass

How can the principles of the Constitution be used as a political compass in judging the laws, orders, and behaviors emanating from our current governments and leaders?

From the principles discussed in the previous chapter, the following four point summary can be used to evaluate a government law or order to determine if it is Constitutional and worthy of obedience. If the inner Constitutional Compass reveals the law or order to be immoral, obedience is not good—following that law is an act of moral cowardice that contributes to the death of the Kid.

The Four Points of the Constitutional Inner Moral Compass dictate a law must:

> 1) be passed by representatives elected in an open and transparently honest election

> 2) respect limits on government power and divisions of federal, state, local, and individual sovereignty

> 3) respect the God-given rights and Judeo-Christian conscience of the people

> 4) treats each person equally and respect the minority

A couple cases from current affairs will be used as a "compass course" to train a person in the skill of using this inner moral Compass.

SAVE THE KID!

Using the Compass - Case One: House Bill 1

The first case is bill HB-1 "The For the People Act."[xlii] It is a House Bill introduced in 2021 after Joe Biden was installed. The numbering of the bill proclaims its importance to House Leader Nancy Pelosi and the 168 Democrat co-sponsors of the bill. The bill is 880 pages of Democrat wish-list control over every detail of every election in the country, including requirements such as:

- early voting two weeks before the election occurs (p.182)

- no use of voter ID, must accept a person's word or a signature (p. 47)

- every voter can receive a mail-in ballot and no ID check is allowed (p. 48)

- every college must establish a "Campus Vote Coordinator" and office (p. 240)

- all college students are to be registered to vote (p. 241)

- all driver license applicants are to be registered to vote (p. 106)

- not allowed to prohibit same day voter registration (p. 84)

- not allowed to prohibit curbside voting (p. 277)

- add penalties for the crime of saying a voter must be eligible (p.142)

- restoration of voting rights for every felon (p.158)

- prohibit campaign information sharing with foreign power (but no evidence of "agreement or formal collaboration" is needed) (p.585)

Many times this bill makes noble claims of promoting election integrity. Who could possibly object to such things as the government mandating election registration offices at a college? Well, the following questions are a few which come to mind about this bill. Why aren't every church, veterans' organization, or retirement home listed for mandatory registration? Many states give driver licenses to illegal aliens, how is the requirement for citizenship going to be protected? If you aren't required to show evidence, how difficult would it be to falsely accuse and convict someone of sharing information with a foreign power?

Despite the rhetoric, the bill is clearly intended to create a closed, corruption-enabling election system, where election uncertainty is the rule. Since no one knows where the votes came from and who cast the votes, there is no way to detect election cheating.

This is in contrast to an open and transparently honest election system where anyone can see who voted and where the votes came from. There can be no suspicion or stench of fraud, because the election was conducted so anyone and everyone could see its operation.

SAVE THE KID!

What does the Compass say about this proposed HB-1 law?

The Constitution says "Congress may at any time by Law make or alter such Regulations"[xliii] about Federal elections, so it clearly has some legislative authority.

However, HB-1 is a law written to destroy the heart of the American experiment as given in Compass point (1)—the placing of political power in the voice of the people.

If this law is written to destroy the heart of America, then why would you ever obey it?

If you believe this law should be obeyed, are you saying that officials in red States and red counties should dutifully implement all 880 pages to ensure an open and transparently honest election *never again occurs* in America? How does their oath to support and defend the Constitution require them to drive a dagger into the heart of the Constitution? How does it require one to kill the Kid?

When placed into contraposition with Leftist actions, this mindset of destructive wrongful obedience on the Right can drive one crazy. To this day the State of California refuses to follow and support Federal immigration law.[xliv] Their inner moral compass of a socialist utopia where there are no national borders, where all the world is equal, and no nation claims distinction or uniqueness overrules a duly passed law—and hardly a squawk is heard! Of course not. The legacy press and most of our self-proclaimed elitists, see the Left's utopian compass as superior to the law, their disobedience is righteous and virtuous.

The absurd "moral" compass of the Left that is used to destroy America is seemingly universally accepted, and patriots cannot even find within themselves the courage to use the Compass of the Constitution to judge and refuse a law that destroys elections in order to get off the sidewalk and save America.

Using the Compass - Case Two: The January 6th Rally

The second case covers the actions of the Department of Justice and the FBI in using the legal system to handle the participants of the January 6th, 2021 rally in Washington DC. (A later chapter will use the Compass to talk generally about the overall morality of the Rally itself.)

I participated in that Rally. I took the subway to the mall on the morning of the 6th, and stood around for hours at the area of the Washington Monument, chatting with people while waiting for President Trump to speak. Some of the people I talked with were of Vietnamese descent and had come as a group to wave the yellow and red flag of South Vietnam. I knew they had an intense personal reason to see the preservation of American freedom and to support the will of the people in honest elections. President Trump spoke for over an hour about the travesty of the election and all the fraud that occurred in the swing States.

My reaction was that of boredom, and the folks around me appeared to feel the same. The fact of the matter is, all of the attendees at the Rally knew of this fraud already—that is why we crossed the country to appear at a "Stop the Steal" rally. My thought at the time was, well at least the uninformed parts of the country are hearing the President's speech and are

SAVE THE KID!

finally learning of this fraud. Not so. Later at home, I shared that thought with other conservatives. They told me that as soon as President Trump started speaking, the legacy media cut away from him.

After the speech, the crowd started walking up to the Capitol Building. It's a long way, and I am not a fast walker. My knees bothered me enough that I stopped a couple of times to sit down. Many thousands were in front of me on the main path, so I worked my way to the south and came up on the side of the steps leading up to the building.

As I came up to the building, two things struck me with overwhelming irony and filled me with indignation. First, all of the lawn around the Capitol was fenced off with metal T-posts and plastic netting and had "Keep off the Grass" signs. Second, the guards where I was, who were manning the other side of the bicycle racks used to cordon off the building at the bottom of the stairs, appeared to be the Capitol tour guides! Two of the guards where I stood were young ladies wearing blue bomber jackets. None of the guards on the south of the building had helmets, shields, gloves, or any type of crowd control equipment.

So this is the way obedience now works in America! No politician or judge will do a *thing* when some secret cabal lusting after political power commits massive election fraud and installs a mumbling puppet with early onset dementia, setting at defiance the most fundamental laws of our land, stabbing at the heart of America, and destroying the voice of the people. A million energized citizens arrive to complain about it and the powers-that-be are so nonchalantly confident that the citizens will obey, they put up "Keep off the Grass" signs and send out the *tour guides*! This struck me as a recreation of the worst parts of the world before America, a set of do-what-you-want rules for the nobles and a set of restrictive rules for the peasant rabble.

So you know what I did? I grabbed a bicycle rack and started pushing and pulling on it, with the goal in mind of crossing the line defended by the guards, to assist in waving the American flag on the steps of the Capitol.

When I put my hands on the rack, no one else in my area was doing anything but standing around. At no time before or after my actions at the line did I see anyone in my area attack a guard, or even scream or curse at them. I thought that breaking the line in this area would flank the more densely packed guards at my far left, who stood at the bottom of the stairs blocking the main steps up the Capitol, trading shots of mace spray with protesters.

But for me, it was over very quickly. Within the first minutes of grappling with the bicycle rack, an officer in a white shirt came around from behind a guard on the front line and hit me with a blast of burning liquid squarely in my eyes. It would be no exaggeration to compare it to being hit with an acid attack. My eyes and the skin on my face burned as if on fire. After the shock of that hit, I remember someone offering me water bottles in order for me to wash my eyes.

Later, when I watched the FBI arrest video,[xlv] it was a total mystery to me how it showed that the bicycle rack barrier had disappeared. All I remembered was stumbling and bumping around with stinging, blurry eyes until someone who noticed my inability to see, reached out and pulled me away from the action at the line.

My eyes and face continued to burn as I walked away. That burning spray wiped me out for the rest of the day. I left the area feeling like a totally useless failure, like a geezer with bad knees too weak to help break the line and allow patriots up the steps.* I sat on a curb trying to recover enough that I could take the subway back to the hotel for a shower to try and scrub it off. The one bright spot during that time, which caused me to laugh while I sat, was the announcement of someone looking at the news on his phone that a guy had put his feet up on Nancy Pelosi's desk. I ended the day at the hotel, and after a *lot* of scrubbing in the shower, going to bed with eyes and face that still stung as if burned in a fire.

And that was it. I went home the next morning, the whole ordeal was over. Or so I thought.

Sometime around February or March, I started hearing from friends that the FBI had made a video of me and it was on YouTube and their Most Wanted website.

Then on April 25th, 2021, while my wife and I were in our Sunday clothes on the way to church, multiple sheriff cars and unmarked vehicles with FBI agents pulled us over and arrested me. No one bothered to read the charges against me as they handcuffed me and stuffed me (yes *stuffed*—some five-foot skinny bureaucrat designed those seats) into a squad car, but my wife was shown paperwork where she saw two counts of "walking on the grass" among the other charges that include assault.

---

*Watching the FBI video greatly improved my spirits in this regard. I did not remember that the bicycle rack was gone and that I had made an attempt to break through the guards' line of control.

READING THE COMPASS

At the time of this writing, it has been eight months since my arrest. I have had three Federal hearings, and had four more hearings scheduled and then postponed by the government. The last hearing held on Zoom had nine charges* read against me—although the "walking on the grass" has been spruced up to scary-sounding trespass charges. Probably the threatened years in the Federal Penitentiary would add up to 50 years.

There will be more to be said about the January 6th Rally later. But for now, the point of this part of the story is *we live ten miles outside of Portland, Oregon.*

For over a year and a half, night after night, I have seen violent Leftists calling themselves "anti-fascists" or "antifa" dressed in black lay waste to what used to be the beautiful, clean City of Roses, attacking not only local buildings and officers, but also the downtown Federal buildings and Federal officers. It is such a regular occurrence that I make the tongue-in-cheek statement that the Portland News channels are the only outlets in the country where a regular riot segment comes on every night after the weather. It's hard to find a thread of logical motivation for these riots, but as near as I can tell, it is that anyone who doesn't believe the "system" is racist and needs to be torn down is a fascist who deserves to be attacked.

During these riots, dozens of officers have been sent to the hospital with severe injuries as they have been assaulted with clubs, bricks, lasers, fire bombs, chemicals, and explosives. While I was in a holding cell in the downtown Federal Building, I asked my jailer how many "antifa" rioters he had seen. Was it hundreds, scores, tens? His answer was "zero."

---

*Five of the charges contain the words, "did forcibly assault, resist, oppose, impede, intimidate, and interfere with an officer and employee of the United States." The other four deal with trespass in the Capitol area.

It would be nice if the so-called intelligentsia of the Right would stop saying patently stupid things like, "the Capitol Hill rioters are only getting the justice they deserve." No, the treatment of the participants of the January 6th Rally has nothing to do with American justice. Using the legal system as a weapon to target political opponents with extreme force, while ignoring the violence of those on its side, is a sure sign the system is nothing more than a kangaroo court of oppression like those used by the German and Soviet socialists.[xlvi]

This does not even seem hard to figure out. If walking with a flag in the Capitol Building gets you six months of solitary confinement without trial, while fire-bombing Federal buildings and officers in Portland get you an FBI free pass, something is wrong.

If it violates Compass point (4), equal application of the law, it is all a fraud and is a sure sign of suppression and tyranny. In a legal system interested in being called American, hundreds of violent rioters in Portland would have been prosecuted and put in jail, and the Federal government would have simply sent me a $300 fine in the mail for disturbing the peace at a protest.

We have now used the Constitutional moral Compass to make broad judgments of some current events, but, the most important use of the Constitutional inner moral Compass is in making one's own individual choices. Examples of this type of compass reading are given in the next chapters.

SAVE THE KID!

V. Being a Moral Actor

SAVE THE KID!

Chapter 15 - I Don't Do That

The first use of the Constitutional moral Compass is to have an inner guide that leads to good and moral individual decisions and actions by refusing to engage in assaults on the freedoms of America. Obeying laws and orders that violate the Constitution is an act of joining the mob to attack the Kid. Without the inner moral Compass for guidance to refuse such acts, you will end up participating in the destruction of the Kid.

In today's world, the flurry of medical mandates from government leaders in response to COVID-19 provides a seemingly endless list of items that need to be evaluated with an inner moral Compass. This chapter will use these items as a compass course to train a patriot in the use of their inner Constitutional moral Compass.

Here is a list of some of these medical mandates:

1. Officials and judges can declare that a pandemic is a reason to use unauthorized edicts to violate laws passed by the legislature and can dictate universal mail-in ballots so elections become closed and corruption-enabled.

2. The governor in my home state of Oregon can use a 28-day Emergency Power clause in the State Constitution to issue orders and mandates for over a year and a half. Governors from other States can do the same. Incredibly, only the South Dakota governor issued medical advisories, all the other governors

issued mandates—deciding the people in their States should be commanded like peasants, instead of advised as fellow citizens.

3. The Federal government can now make medical edicts that override laws passed by State governments.

4. The government now has all power over you. Their power to make health decisions, which contain life and death risk evaluations, is now greater than your individual free will.

5. Your property rights are disposable. The lifetime struggle to build a small business can be destroyed.

6. Your right to assemble is forbidden. People are ordered to stay home or travel is restricted. You have no right to rejoice at a wedding, to mourn at a funeral, to gather for a family reunion. You are not allowed to eat, exercise, or use any other public facility except under government authorization.

7. The government controls your religious worship. It can close down your church. It can dictate how the Lord's supper is to be administered, whether you are allowed to sing hymns, and where you can sit in the pews.

8. Leftist riots that destroy American cities are deemed medically safe, while any gathering to complain against medical tyranny is called a super-spreader event.

9. Stores owned by mega-corporations are safe for shopping, while small businesses require shutdown and destruction.

10. The elite rulers and nobles of the American empire can vacation, party, and gather without masks and other medical restrictions. Moms who take their stir-crazed children to an outdoor park, and other *peasant rabble* need to be rounded up by law enforcement and taken to prison.

11. While on the other hand, violent convicted prisoners need to be released for their protection.

Using the Compass to evaluate the mandates made by governments in the name of medical emergency is not too difficult, since they violate every one of the four points on the Constitutional moral Compass!

Compass Point 1 - voice of the people in open elections—violated by 1, 2

Compass Point 2 - limited powers of government and division of sovereignty—violated by 3, 4

Compass Point 3 - inalienable rights of the people—violated by 5, 6, 7

Compass Point 4 - equally applied and respect to the minority—violated by 8, 9, 10, 11

SAVE THE KID!

It took just a short look at the Compass to clearly see that every one of the four compass points indicates that all of these medical mandates are furious and direct assaults on the Kid. A person who complies with these orders (even if they become laws) cannot claim to love America and love the Constitution as they pick up a crow bar and participate in beating the Kid.

The following are ways that a person with a Constitutional inner moral Compass would behave in the face of the medical mandates:

> - A citizen would not confront other citizens over a mask decision. He would not call the government to snitch on them. He would respect individuals making their own medical choices.

> - A manager or HR person would refuse to carry out orders to fire, fine, or punish an employee over these mandates.

> - An elected official would refuse to fire doctors, nurses, EMT, police, and firefighters for making their own medical decisions, especially since that action would cripple their community and leave citizens in danger.

> - County officials would refuse to implement corruption enabling election orders, often given in spite of the law, excused with "cuz pandemic."

> - A police officer or deputy would refuse to harass and arrest citizens to enforce these mandates.

I DON'T DO THAT

- A National Guard member would refuse an order to activate that enables a government to enforce its tyranny and to fire and oppress its citizens.

- A business owner would not shut down a business. He would not pay any fine imposed. He would not confront customers over masks or vaccination.

Toward the end of October 2021, the owner of a fast food store for In-N-Out Burger in San Francisco made a perfect use of the Constitutional inner moral Compass.[xlvii] When given vaccine orders by the city of San Francisco the owner replied,

> "We refuse to become the vaccination police for any government. We fiercely disagree with any government dictate that forces a private company to discriminate against customers who choose to patronize their business. This is a clear government overreach."

It's scary to see this and realize there seems to be exactly *one* business owner in all of San Francisco with the courage to be a moral actor and say, "I don't work for you, and I don't obey unconstitutional orders."

Americans used to know a word that describes a country where everyone works for the government—the word is *communist*.

One article about this situation commented that the county health department acted after getting multiple complaints on their 311 snitch line.[xlviii] Sounds about right. In communist East Germany, one out of three people were listed as working as government snitches.

SAVE THE KID!

In a society composed of people with moral courage, this In-N-Out Burger store would not stand alone. County health employees would refuse to issue shutdown orders and fines. Police and county deputies would refuse to harass and arrest the workers. Judges would refuse to grant collection actions for fines. In short, instead of everyone "just doing their job," resulting in a massive attack on the Kid, there would be a wannabe tyrant with a foam-flecked mouth standing alone, screaming orders—and no one would be listening.

In a society with moral confusion, people follow immoral laws and file lawsuits. They will not use the moral Compass on their own, they need someone to tell them what to do. Presumably, the hope is some judge will tell them it is okay not to beat on the Kid. However, given the performance of American courts (up to and including the Supreme Court) refusing to even look at evidence during the 2020 election fraud, be prepared to receive the duly considered judicial order to pick up a club and start beating.

Who could have foreseen two years ago, that a bad flu would cause world leaders to engage in an all-out assault on the individual liberty that is at the pinnacle of accomplishments of the Western world?

Americans using the Constitution as a Compass should know better. Americans should have an advantage over others in assessing this tyranny done in the name of medicine. Our Constitutional Compass is screaming and flashing red that this is the wrong path, and no patriot should be proceeding down it.

I DON'T DO THAT

Adding to what one *should not* do, the next chapter expands on what an American patriot *should* be doing to protect the Kid.

SAVE THE KID!

Chapter 16 - I Should Do That

In the last chapter, we learned how to apply the Constitution as an inner moral Compass to our individual actions in order to refuse participation in attacks on America. That is a correct first step, but a freedom-loving American who wants to do what is moral and right should also step forward to protect the Kid from the mob. Recall that the allegory helps us to see clearly that not doing anything to help the Kid can also be a blatantly immoral act.

It is possible a broad awakening of Americans refusing unconstitutional orders and laws may shock those who are acting as *rulers,* not *representatives,* to mend their ways. It is also just as possible these rulers will double down and respond by expanding their despotic tendencies and engaging in even greater tyranny and coercion.

The actions of pushing back against tyranny in this chapter are staged to be in proportional response to the coercion and force used to promote tyranny and attack American freedoms. But before beginning that discussion, it needs to be said how far this goes—what is at the end of this tit for tat, this tyrannical force versus patriotic response?

To see how this can end up, we need to address the often heard shibboleth that an American conservative or patriot would "never commit violence." I guess somebody forgot to tell that to George Washington. In a functioning American legal system with Constitutional laws, proper enforcement, and equal justice for all, that statement would be true, but it is certainly not true when facing a tyrannical system.

In a tyrannical system, refuting violence is exactly the same as saying that you believe you and your family should be slaves. History is chock-full of tyrants who were more than willing to use torture and murder to make people slaves. Do you really think none of those wannabe tyrants exist now in our time? If you fail to see the morality of using force to defend your family and freedoms from such evil, then you are displaying the same stunning level of moral ignorance as the Silicon Rock Creature discussed in Chapter 4.

Simply reading the Declaration of Independence shows without question that the American Founders were concerned with not *if* but *when* force is required against tyranny. Americans have a simple rule about this: if you are a tyrant who tries to take away our freedom, we will kill you. *Sic semper tyrannis*—"Thus be it ever to tyrants," was a motto of the American Revolution.

The Founders also taught us when to begin shooting. In 1775, when a small number of militia men on the Lexington town green faced down the British regulars, it was because the British had come to *get the guns*. Our ancestors understood why every tyranny needs to have the population defenseless, and it is a point of no return. In light of the events of the 20th century, it can also be said that the point of no return has been reached when the government begins mass round ups of political enemies to put in camps.

Well, that discussion was heavy. Although the American Founding is under terrible assault, I have faith we have not reached a point of no return, and the Kid can be restored to safety out of the street. Let us go back now to the start and talk about non-violent ways that one can use to begin to push back against the America-hating mob bent on its destruction.

I SHOULD DO THAT

Let's take the example of a restaurant owner who refuses to enforce unconstitutional government edicts. The government sends a health inspector and some deputies, moral cowards just doing their jobs, to shut the place down.

The following non-violent actions spring to mind. These examples are all non-violent, but can come with consequences (legal and otherwise), that make choosing to do something to save the Kid a moral decision requiring courage that must be seriously considered by each individual.

- Patriots could be on hand *en masse* to support the owner with a tidal wave of patronage.

- A worker in the sheriff's office or health office could send an early warning of the enforcement action.

- The roads in the area could be congested with vehicles to prevent government access.

- People could crowd in front of the officials and link arms to impede their movement into the building.

- Cars could be placed to prevent official vehicles from leaving—with tow truck operators refusing to be in the service of petty tyrants.

- The air could be let out of the tires of the officials' vehicles.

The above list of non-violent actions took just a few minutes to compile, and with a little imagination, many more actions could be listed. With such non-violent impediments, the officials who snap their heels and throw up their arm in salute and agree to tyrannical orders would be *lucky* to harass one business owner in a full day. Their threats would be meaningless in the face of many owners standing up with the support of American patriots.

While officials remain non-violent in enforcing their unconstitutional edicts, there are many such ways of non-violent resistance. Blocking officials, blocking vehicles, disabling vehicles and equipment, etc. Those on the Left have no basis to be critical of this resistance and to get their panties in a wad and start wailing about how wrong this is. For over sixty years our rulers and self-proclaimed elitists have had no problem with, and have even given encouragement to, the Left doing these actions and more during protests in service to their bogus, utopian moral compass guiding them to tear down American society and history. Those on the Right need to recognize that following a true Constitutional moral Compass to resist those engaging in assaulting the Kid is a good and moral behavior.

State and county officials also can take steps to defend the Kid from assault and keep their oath to uphold the Constitution. Recall that point (2) of the Compass says that the Constitution provides for each level of government to have its own sovereignty. It is a good first step to not obey unconstitutional orders, but elected officials have a duty to do more—to protect the people they serve. Is it acceptable to have the FBI conducting police state roundups in your jurisdiction, throwing a non-violent selfie taker into jail for two months with no trial,[xlix] and threatening to do the same to irate parents at a school board meeting?

I SHOULD DO THAT

If attacks on the American Constitution ratchet up in violence, the patriotic response should ratchet up as well. No hypothetical examples will be suggested for responses to violent provocations, as there are plenty of hack government lawyers who are just waiting to cry incitement. However, it turns out there is a perfect, recent historical example to examine: the January 6th, 2021 "Stop the Steal" rally in Washington DC.

What did the patriots at the January 6th Rally actually *do* in response to a presidential election being stolen? I'm not asking what nonsensical insurrection stories the media hyped up, or what sanctimonious fears politicians and guards cried about (and in a crowd of a million or more, I'm not saying that there may not have been some violent outliers, or some number of FBI agitators). I'm just asking, in general, *what happened*?

The patriots not only had a rally, they *protested*. They walked on the grass, they crossed the government's line of control, and with each successful movement up the Capitol steps to wave the American flag, a cheer would rise up from the crowd. That is what I saw on the front line and as I sat on the curb recovering from a chemical attack, looking through red and swollen eyes up at the Capitol.

There is one thing Democrat politicians and their allies in the legacy media are right about—the January 6th Rally was an unprecedented event, the likes of which have not happened since the time of the Civil War. The Rally was the first time since the abominable Dred Scott ruling that patriots and Republicans in large numbers actually used an inner moral Compass to get off the sidewalk and to respond with disobedience.

The Left has been using their socialist utopian moral compass for over sixty years to instigate protests and riots of disobedience, and they immediately recognized the significance of this protest. I have yet to see any conservative or Republican commentator or writer who has even a glimmer of real understanding about how important this was.

Consciously or not, perhaps just reacting instinctively as Americans, the Rally goers sent a clear message to the secret cabal who corrupted and stole a presidential election and who installed the puppet Biden, the oligarchs who paid for it, and the deep-state politicians and judges who did nothing to stop it. The message was this: you will not get obedience from patriotic Americans after having just stabbed a dagger into the heart of America.

In sum, the January 6th Rally was a perfect response to a violent attack on the Kid. It was a shot across the bow of the Washington DC deep-state elites, and their reaction shows that the warning shot was seen and clearly understood. This is why government apparatchiks are frantically acting like king men, imitating their tyrannical icons of old, and are using the Department of Justice and the FBI to busily cut off peasant heads and put them on pikes in front of the castle gate. All the better to scare the deplorable peasant rabble off the streets and back into submission.

We have discussed the things we should not do, and the things we should do to save the Kid. But the America-hating mob is enraged and determined to kill the Constitution and the Republic. How can we have the courage to be a moral actor and listen to our Constitutional inner moral Compass? This is discussed in the next and final chapter.

Chapter 17 – Finding the Courage

Using a Constitutional moral Compass to do what is right will not be easy. How does one find the courage to do what is right and to be a moral actor?

To regularly use the Constitutional moral Compass, you must first have it firmly rooted in your mind. The Compass is listed at the top of Chapter 14, and the four points of the Compass are summarized here. Learn them and commit them to memory:*

>(1) voice of the people in open elections

>(2) limited powers of government and division of sovereignty

>(3) inalienable rights of the people

>(4) equally applied and respect to the minority

Then use the points of the Compass to evaluate every news story, politician statement, law, or government order you see. The first step to being a moral actor is to see the proper path clearly and without confusion.

The next step is to use the clarity of vision given by the Constitutional Compass to *not do evil*, as discussed in Chapter 15. You must have the moral courage to refuse to participate in actions that are attacks on American freedoms.

---

* A file for a wallet-size card with these Constitutional Compass points is here: savethekid.com/book/compass_card.pdf

If you cannot muster this amount of courage to defend your country, then your expressions of love for America and its history and heritage are empty and hollow phrases. Likewise, something I have often thought about, how can I say I love my children and grandchildren if I fearfully surrender my free will and obey orders and laws that are unconstitutional? As the allegory teaches, giving in to this fear is exactly the same as joining the mob to attack the Kid and helping to destroy the freedom and prosperity of America for future generations.

After you have some experience in refusing actions that violate the Constitutional Compass, your courage will grow and you can start to consider the more difficult actions of defending America as discussed in Chapter 16. The legacy media and the rulers of the deep-state want you to think that you will be alone as you step up to take actions to protect America and its Founding—but that is not the truth.

The truth of the matter is you, and most people, have an inherent tendency to want to do what is right (while sometimes failing to heed that tendency). I know of no tyrannical leader or ideology that recruited populations to further its evil that did so by preaching "let's go be evil." Rather the people were deceived into believing that going down the wrong path was the right thing to do by means of a false compass. The prime examples of this in our day are the racial superiority bogus compass of the National Socialists of Germany, and the utopia bogus compass of the Soviet Socialists and the American Left.

Because most people want to do what is right, you will find you will not stand alone. Often it just takes one person to stand up and be the first to do what is right to get people pointed in the right direction. In plain terms, it takes a leader.

Start by reaching out to the people around you who have similar beliefs. Start in your local community to band together with like-minded people, then grow your moral courage to do what is right by turning around your neighborhood, your town, your county, and your state to protect the Kid and to become bulwarks of the United States Constitution.

The urge to be courageous is much less common than the urge to blend in and hunker down. Perhaps it is from thousands of years of tyrants cutting off the heads of anyone who first raised their voice to protest. Regardless, with a courageous leader calling out a clear choice between good and evil, many if not most people will follow.

The assault that many people will face for standing up for the Kid will be in the form of comments from the vicious gutter of Twitter and the inquisition monks from the Church of the Crazy College Pinheads (CCCP)* who are attempting to stamp out anyone who they see as heretics. Comments from such people, crowing about their knowledge and superiority while following a bogus compass down the pathway to evil, should be ignored and given the disdain they deserve.

But comments on the internet from anonymous strangers are not the only price one can pay for getting in the street and standing up for the Kid, things can get much harder. Choosing the moral path can lead to more concrete persecution, such as loss of family relationships, friendships,

---

*My term for the "woke," coincidentally the same initials as the former Soviet Empire

or a job. I'm beginning to have some understanding about these sudden life changes, since this year has seen:

- being on the FBI Wanted list,

- being thrown naked into jail,

- having three Federal Court hearings with no end in sight,

- retiring five years earlier than I had planned, being worried that there might be members of the CCCP in the upper management structure of Intel,

- and, finding out that our son turned me in to the FBI.

My wife was informed of the last item in an email from him announcing the cutting of all contact and family ties. To Myra and me, this information was the private business of the family and didn't need to be public. Then while this book was undergoing editing, an article from NBC News was found, which required that a statement seen there should be publicly addressed:[1]

> *The FBI said Reed Christensen of Oregon, accused of assaulting officers on the Capitol's lower west terrace, was identified with the help of his son.*

Gee, that was nice, FBI and NBC News. I'm not sure I understand what knowing who turned me in has got to do with anything. But it does explain the aerial map my wife saw at my arrest, which had annotations that could only come from someone who had been physically on the property. For now we deal with a broken family by having faith in a truth that my lawyer defending me in Federal Court points out, "family relationships are dynamic—and they can change."

It's not only family divisions that are tearing at people as the assault on the Kid intensifies, for the political gulag has come to America[li]—with hundreds arrested and charged, and dozens in jail undergoing unlawful pretrial detention, beatings, holding in cells covered with sewage, withholding food, withholding medical care, hindering access to a lawyer, and so forth. After six months, the word of this behavior is starting to leak out of the cover the government has tried to put up. The journalist Julie Kelly at *American Greatness* has been one of the people who has doggedly uncovered and reported on this abuse.[lii] Unbelievably, it took until the end of October before a Washington DC District Court judge ordered a US marshal to make a snap inspection to confirm this treatment, and to call out the Federal legal system for its abuse[liii] (with the judge still being too weasely to admit that those who attended the January 6th Rally are political prisoners).

If it still hasn't hit you, let me just state the obvious and say that having a political gulag in America is a big deal and it makes one wonder if the Kid hasn't already been murdered.

This is not the first time in history that good people have been in perilous times. At one of the freedom rallies in Oregon, a pastor giving a prayer shared a scripture that resonates with the zeitgeist of our time:

SAVE THE KID!

For we wrestle not against flesh and blood, but against principalities, against powers, against the rulers of the darkness of this world, against spiritual wickedness in high places. *

What can one person do against such evil?

Yes there is tremendous evil, but there is good that pushes back. One encouraging thing, which I have realized by standing with the Kid against the mob, is when terrible things happen, like the pain of seeing your family ties torn up, there can also be amazingly good things that happen as well.

When the local news media got wind of my arrest and broadcast my name and picture on the evening news, there was a phone caller who asked, "Does Reed Christensen live here?" When asked who they were, they immediately hung up.

This weird call was extremely distressing to my wife whose gentle nature had already been rocked by my arrest, and who now had visions of Portland rioters streaming onto our property. I told her that I would take the tractor and some tools to the end of our half mile rural driveway and install a chain to block the road to keep cars from coming up close. This was the first time I had attempted to work outside since having my stroke, and Myra was quite worried about me doing that. While I took the tractor and tools to the end of the driveway, she took the car and went to see if a neighbor would come to help.

She was gone longer than I expected, but I was not working very fast and not much had been done when she came driving

---

Ephesians 6:12 King James version of the Bible

up with several pickup trucks following behind. A neighbor who runs a farm jumped out, listened to my plan to chain the road, and said, "No, we're going to do something different." Several other men came from the trucks with a hole auger, thick pine posts, and metal T-posts. The neighbor got everyone busy with work assignments, including sending one man back to his farm for a steel cable, a lock, and fastening hardware. In no time at all a sturdy barrier that was easy to lock and unlock was in place. It was an amazing, uplifting experience to learn how much our neighbors would help and support us.

Myra later told me that during her conversation to ask the neighbors at the farm for help, she told the wife that she thought we should move out of leftist Oregon and go away to Montana, the state where Myra was raised. The wife quizzically looked at her, and simply said, "Why would you let them drive you out of your home?" Myra said at that moment she felt darkness and dread, fear and anxiety just physically wash out of her. She said it was like a heavenly voice immediately cleansed and lightened her mind and soul. Since being caught up in the persecutions of the Department of Justice and the FBI, I have written down a couple of pages of such miracles and tender mercies as these that have occurred to buoy us up. The only logical explanation I can come up with is God sends down special help to people having troubles because they showed the moral courage to stand up for what is right.

Also, on the list of good that will stand up for the Kid, I firmly believe there is a God in Heaven who doesn't want to see the American Founding destroyed. He blessed this land against tyranny and sent his brightest and most courageous sons and daughters at the right time and to the right place so

SAVE THE KID!

they could found a new era of freedom and prosperity for all of His children in the entire world.

I'm guessing He has done the same thing again—He has sent the bright and courageous people America needs at its time of peril, and you are one of them. He will give us the strength, the means, and the knowledge to stand for what is right and to save the Kid.

There are some things we have to do. We have to take the first step in faith, to step forward and to do what is right when things look the most awful. And when the whole nefarious rascality of evil comes down on us, we need to get on our knees and ask for His help.

I would add a couple other things that one could do as we pray for help in this spiritual battle, things that have proven a great benefit to me:

> - Use the power of the Fast, as explained in the Bible in Isaiah 58. On your worship day once a month, skip breakfast and lunch and donate at least the money for those meals to a charity that feeds, clothes, or houses the poor. Then go visit some family members you haven't seen in a while.

> - Don't participate in the coarsening of America's spiritual fabric by using the Lord's name in vain. In this contest of good and evil we need the Lord's help. Giving respect to this Commandment is a good way to show we are earnest in our request for His help.

Finally, I would attempt to give one last motivation to do what is right, no matter the cost, by pointing out that you cannot "obey" yourself out of tyranny, as a good friend pointed out. Once you and your nation start down the path of obeying tyrannical and evil orders, it puts you on a path leading to horrors that now seem unimaginable. Yet the history of humanity is full of such examples, including the tens of millions murdered in the recent 20th century.

Picture yourself on the great and last Judgment Day, when each person will individually stand before the Lord and Judge of all. Will you be standing there with the blood of America on your hands, since you cowardly obeyed immoral orders and participated in killing America? Is your plan for that Day to put yourself in the long line with all those who are going to try out the excuse, "I was just following orders" or "I was just doing my job"?

Or, will you be able to stand tall and unashamed, as a person of moral courage who took the Constitutional Compass in hand, got off the sidewalk, and helped to Save the Kid?

SAVE THE KID!

For More Information

Please visit this site to gain current information about my efforts to urge the use of the Constitution as a Moral Compass and to learn about my status with the Federal courts.

savethekid.com

Please consider visiting this site which I discovered while writing this book. The site is a project of Jim Hoft, *"for the benefit of the public and to provide sunshine and publicity to the scores of political prisoners wrongfully imprisoned as a result of the protest on January 6th."*

Jim looks to have spent hundreds of hours compiling the names and status' of those under Federal indictment. By including this link I hope readers will find someone who can use their help.

americangulag.org

What Did You Think ?

Thank You For Reading My Book!

I would really appreciate your feedback about this book and what impact it may have had on your views and support of America and its Constitution.

Please leave me an honest review on your purchase site letting me know what you thought of the book.

Thanks so much!
Reed K. Christensen
SavetheKid.com

Endnotes

i The following arrest, jailing, and Hearing account is taken from the author's notes written the same week as the arrest.
ii The accuracy of the following Hearing dialog confirmed from Court transcript – USA vs Christensen, No. 3:21-mj-00094 April 26, 2021 Portland, Oregon
iii See an image of a newspaper photo about the rally here: savethekid.com/book/rally_photo.jpg
iv Star Trek, Season 3, Episode 22 – The Savage Curtain
v https://en.wikipedia.org/wiki/History_of_Nauvoo,_Illinois
vi https://www.beautifulnauvoo.com/nauvoo-during-the-mormon-period-(1839-1846).html
vii https://rsc.byu.edu/vol-19-no-2-2018/power-principles#_edn1
viii https://constitutionallaw.regent.edu/preserving-a-constitution-designed-for-a-moral-and-religious-people/
ix https://corporatemachiavelli.com/societies-high-trust-and-low-trust/
x https://en.wikipedia.org/wiki/Code_of_Hammurabi
xi Ibid., Code_of_Hammurabi
xii Ibid., Code_of_Hammurabi
xiii http://www.darrinqualman.com/2000-years-of-economic-growth/ (I have not been able to locate the original video, but the chart looked like the one at this site.)
xiv https://www.history.com/topics/american-revolution/american-revolution-history
xv https://www.powerlineblog.com/archives/2021/02/remembering-mr-lincoln-10.php
xvi https://www.history.com/this-day-in-history/adolf-hitler-is-named-chancellor-of-germany
xvii http://nuremberg.law.harvard.edu/transcripts/ page 8540
xviii https://www.history.com/topics/vietnam-war/my-lai-massacre-1
xix The Gulag Archipelago, by Aleksandr-Solzhenitsyn
xx MiG Pilot, The Final Escape of Lt. Belenko, by John Barron
xxi Mao's Great Famine, The History of China's Most Devastating Catastrophe 1958-1962, by Victor Dikotter
xxii The Killing Fields of Cambodia, Surviving a Living Hell, by

	Sokphal Din
xxiii	http://nuremberg.law.harvard.edu
xxiv	Ordinary Men, Reserve Police Battalion 101 and the Final Solution in Poland, Christopher R. Browning, February 2017
xxv	Ibid., Ordinary Men, pg 57
xxvi	https://www.oregon.gov/boli/workers/Pages/covid-vaccine.aspx
xxvii	https://www.oregonlive.com/business/2021/08/oregon-says-people-fired-for-refusing-vaccines-generally-cant-collect-jobless-benefits.html
xxviii	https://stateofreform.com/featured/2021/09/oregon-health-worker-capacity-issues/
xxix	https://www.britannica.com/event/Dred-Scott-decision
xxx	Ibid., Dred Scott
xxxi	https://en.wikiquote.org/wiki/Daniel_Boone
xxxii	The Story of Christianity, The Early Church to the Present Day, Justo L. Gonzalez, pg 40-41
xxxiii	Ibid., The Story of Christianity, pg 41
xxxiv	Ibid., The Story of Christianity, pg 41
xxxv	https://www.bestdegreeprograms.org/features/college-protests-social-movements/
xxxvi	https://www.ushistory.org/us/54f.asp
xxxvii	http://www.ukemonde.com/news/usefulidiot.html
xxxviii	https://www.webster-dictionary.org/definition/federal
xxxix	https://en.wikipedia.org/wiki/European_wars_of_religion
xl	https://en.wikipedia.org/wiki/Bread_and_circuses
xli	https://www.reference.com/history/great-compromise-1787-b16fd894cffc87d6
xlii	https://legiscan.com/US/bill/HB1/2021
xliii	The Constitution, Article I, Section 4
xliv	https://kameli.com/2019/11/02/california-laws-immigrants/
xlv	https://www.youtube.com/watch?v=WIsPjBS9Qzg
xlvi	https://americangulag.org/
xlvii	https://www.sfgate.com/food/article/San-Francisco-In-N-Out-temporarily-closed-16546332.php
xlviii	Ibid., San Francisco In-N-Out
xlix	https://amgreatness.com/2021/08/19/a-life-destroyed-for-parading-at-the-capitol/
l	https://www.nbcnews.com/politics/justice-department/fbi-still-

li   after-worst-worst-capitol-riot-new-arrests-come-n1266580
lii   https://americangulag.org/
https://amgreatness.com/2021/05/17/shawshank-for-january-6-detainees/
https://amgreatness.com/2021/06/10/letters-from-a-d-c-jail/
https://amgreatness.com/2021/07/22/a-january-6-detainee-speaks-out/
https://amgreatness.com/2021/04/07/julie-kelly-and-tucker-carlson-on-the-collapsing-january-6-narrative/
https://amgreatness.com/2021/09/17/joe-bidens-political-prisoners/
liii   https://townhall.com/tipsheet/mattvespa/2021/11/05/dc-jail-stopped-federal-marshals-from-investigating-the-alleged-deplorable-condition-of-january-6-defendants-n2598626

Made in the USA
Middletown, DE
04 December 2023

44570292R00076